LOST & FOUND

lost & found

9 life-changing lessons
about stuff from someone
who lost everything

Helen Chandler-Wilde

CHRONICLE PRISM

MIX
Paper | Supporting
responsible forestry
FSC www.fsc.org   FSC™ C008047

Contents

For where your treasure is, there will your heart be also

Savour no more than 'tis good that you recall.

—*Geoffrey Chaucer, translated by A. S. Kline*

Losing things doesn't just mean losing. . . . When we lose things, we gain things too.

—*Taylor Swift, New York University, 2022*

Prologue

If you could save just one thing from a fire, what would it be? What do you really value the most: your wedding dress, or the last pictures of your parents? A family heirloom, or your watch? Your laptop, or your passport? What one object is so central to who you are that you couldn't live without it?

I wish I had been offered the choice.

Introduction

I had just gotten home when my parents called me into the kitchen and gestured for me to sit down at the table.

I was in my midtwenties and had just gone through a bad breakup, and while I worked out what to do next, I was living out of a few suitcases at my parents' house. It was not just me in limbo: My stuff was too. All of it—furniture, sentimental stuff, books—was packed up in a storage unit. Or at least, it had been. My mother sat down at the table across from me, drew in an awkward breath, and shut her eyes for a moment, as if to shield herself from the situation. "Darling, I've got some . . . some quite bad news. There's been a fire. On New Year's Eve, that storage unit, well . . . everything's gone."

I looked at her, unable to fully understand what she was saying. My father had been lingering further back in the room, but as I turned to him he walked over and laid a hand on my shoulder. I looked again at each of their inscrutable faces, and then started to laugh. "OK, very funny, you almost got me!" I said. "You can stop it now."

The corners of my mother's lips rose up in a smile that could have been, then fell again.

"No, love, it's not a joke," she said, and slid her phone across the table. The screen showed a story on BBC News, with a headline reading "Croydon self-storage destroyed in blaze." I looked at the picture, and yes, that was it.

When I had taken my things there it had been a modern and impersonal warehouse building. At first look, there was something a little severe about it, with its chilly corridors and harsh white lights. But inside the units it was quite different. When the doors opened, they revealed the wondrous mystery of other lives. From just a few glimpses you could weave together a story: I wondered if the man packing away the watercolors and brown furniture had cleared out his mother's house; maybe the young couple storing the cheap wardrobe was about to move abroad.

But the pictures in the news article were very different. The building, a trove of a thousand people's treasures, was now nothing more than a few blackened trunks of steel.

Panic crept up my body, first deadening the sensations in my legs, then tightening my chest, before reaching up to clutch my throat until my head felt light and woozy. My life in suitcases was built on the fragile hope that that storage unit contained: that one day I would leave my parents' house again, one day I wouldn't feel so heartbroken, one day things would return to normal. It felt like the rug had been pulled out from under my feet again and again and again.

I curled my hand tightly around the phone. I had to stop myself from throwing it to the floor.

Without saying anything else, I went upstairs to my temporary room and laid down—on the single bed I had had as a child, not my adult double, which was now a pile of ashes.

Every time I tried to calm down, another item I had lost popped into my head and tears started pricking again. Every single memento, every reminder of the past that I had ever owned, was gone. I had also lost all the practical stuff that I desperately needed: a table, a set of knives and forks, an ironing board. There was also a third category of things that I didn't exactly need, but I really, really liked. The thick blanket I snuggled under on the sofa, the candlesticks I got out when guests came round. All of it, gone.

I called three friends that night. The first comforted me. The second was silent, unsure what to say. The third hyperventilated with me, at first sure that it was a joke, and then sure that it wasn't.

* * *

The next day, I opened my wardrobe and saw a brown moving box marked "RANDOM." Before locking up the storage unit, it had caught my eye and I had pulled it out: I didn't know what was inside but thought it might contain my passport or something else I would need in the coming months.

But I found the passport in my handbag, and given that I couldn't even remember what was in the box, I had never had reason to open it. But after hearing the news, it looked different. It was now the only survivor, a one-of-a-kind antique. With desperate hope for what was inside, I fetched a pair of scissors to cut open the tape across the top.

But I couldn't do it. Yes, if I opened the box, I would find out what I still had, but I would also find out exactly what I had lost. If I kept the box sealed, I could stay in a liminal place where I might have photo albums from my childhood. I might have some postcards from friends, or letters from family. I could pretend that the box contained anything I wanted it to.

I left the box in the wardrobe and shut the door. That was a task for another day.

★ ★ ★

The pain changed over the following weeks and months. I didn't realize it at the time, but I was grieving. One day, I was sitting at my desk at work when I suddenly thought about my coffee table. A few years before, I had hosted a dinner party where a dripping glass of red wine left a ring on its pale pine surface. There was something about that image—the homely familiarity of it, the cozy imperfection—that made me dash to the bathroom to cry in peace.

The strength of this heartbreak surprised me. It seemed rational to be upset about losing the most precious things that reminded me of the past, but a table with a ring on it? I couldn't work out why exactly I felt so sentimental about it, especially when I had been annoyed about the stain at the time.

One evening that spring I was getting ready for a friend's birthday party. I wiggled my way into a tight black dress and went to put on a pair of long silver earrings that I saved for special occasions. I rooted through the suitcases of clothes that I was living out of but I couldn't find them. And then I remembered: They had been in that damn storage container. That fire had even taken my nice earrings. This flash of anger was a new stage of grief. Everything felt so unfair. I had been building myself a nest with my things and it had been snatched away from me.

Occasionally, dark humor helped me to crawl out of the well. To start, there was the fact that the place had burned down on New Year's Eve. "New year, new me!" I would joke, tears still in my eyes. I went round offering my spring-cleaning services to friends, telling them that I had found a very fast, yet very thorough, method to clear out stuff.

And also, I wondered if there was something fitting about the fact that the fire had happened a few months after my ex and I had broken up. Everything we had shared had gone up in smoke, literally! The past—cremated! Was I ready to let go of it all? Absolutely not. But it felt like fate, now, had forced me into getting over it.

It was clear that the stuff I had collected meant much more to me than its strict functionality. I was grieving for the loss of everything that came with it: security, memory, identity, home.

The only people who truly understood were those who were victims of the same fire. We formed a group on social media and used it to talk to each other about the things we had lost.

I cried reading about people who had lost the only copies of photographs of their late parents. I exchanged messages with a man who understood how untethering it was to lose all my books—he had lost a collection of first editions of his favorite author that he had carefully built up over the years.

I spoke to a couple, Demetria and Johannes, about how the fire had robbed them of their careers. Demetria had lost the racks of clothes she'd made over the years as a fashion designer; Johannes lost equipment he'd built up over years as a film composer. And they couldn't have found out in a worse way: On New Year's Eve, they were hosting a party for friends who had flown in from Brazil when they heard about it on the news. Demetria cried that night, and every night for the next three weeks, about their losses. Even now, the pair are careful about looking at old photos in case they see something that was destroyed. It's just too painful.

For Demetria, losing her stuff was such a great shock that she has been forced to leave her designing career behind. "It kind of took something away from it," she told me. "I can't find my inspiration anymore."

Some people grieved for the stuff that helped them remember the past and feel connected to it. Others felt like they had lost things that were important for their sense of identity, and how they showed it to the world. A few people talked about a weird sense of lightness, or possibly insignificance, of going about your life owning so little. And many people were simply reeling from the financial damage of losing the things they needed to make a living.

★ ★ ★

Going through something extreme brought to light how confused and conflicted my feelings about my possessions were. And I'm not the only one. In the Western world, we seem to love and hate our stuff: We buy vast quantities of it, but much of it ends up in landfills shortly after. In the US, stuff abounds to such an extent that the average American throws 81 pounds (36.74 kg) of clothing into landfills every year—equivalent to around 262 T-shirts.[1] Our excesses start early in life too: A decade ago, it was estimated that the average American child gets $6,500 worth of toys in their lifetime.[2] Stuff can also do strange things to our minds, warping our behavior in unpleasant ways. A website called Black Friday Death Count has counted 17 deaths and 125 injuries that have happened since 2006 in shopping centers on the day after Thanksgiving. The headlines that go with the numbers are truly something to behold: "Shirtless man uses belt as a whip outside Vancouver Black Friday sale" in 2016; and, five years earlier, "Girl trampled in Black Friday Wal-Mart rush."[3]

And while sometimes we can get into actual fights over stuff, other times we are indifferent to it. A survey in the United States asked adults to list what they got for Christmas the prior year, and over half couldn't remember a single thing they had received.[4]

Now that I owned almost nothing, I started to think about where all my stuff had come from in the first place. It felt as if collecting stuff in a regimented way, based around life milestones, was the default thing to do. When you start school, you buy a backpack. When you get married, you buy a dress. And on your birthday each year, you get a load of new stuff just to celebrate the fact that you're still here. I had never consciously chosen to amass so much—I was just doing the same thing as everyone else.

Moving in with my boyfriend had been one such milestone. I felt so grown up as we merged our stuff together then went shopping to fill in the gaps. We brought everything home and unpacked it. I lit the tea lights, folded the towels, and made tea with the new kettle. It comforted me to know that we had cupboards full of all the things you're meant to have: spare duvets, Christmas decorations, the manual explaining how the TV worked. Looking at it all made me feel at peace, like we had built a proper home together.

But less than two years later I was unpacking those cupboards and dividing the crockery into two piles. After unfaithfulness and a year of rows, our relationship was over.

In the living room, I picked up the cushions from the sofa. When we'd bought them, I'd imagined us plumping them up around us as we watched films on winter nights, and yet here I was, squashing them down and shoving them into a box. It was shameful, like I'd failed the stuff itself—it had been bought for a life of romantic bliss that I had not been able to achieve. It reminded me of *Beauty and the Beast:* The animated crockery mopes around the empty house, sad that without jolly dinner parties it can't fulfill its purpose.

When you buy something, you make an implicit promise. You are pledging to yourself, and to everyone else who lives on this planet of scant resources, that you will use it. But I was not doing that; I had not held up my end of the bargain.

My parents helped to ferry my belongings to a storage container in south London. After a full day of packing and sorting dozens of boxes and a home's worth of furniture, locking up the storage unit and driving home with just a few suitcases felt freeing. It felt a bit like I was on vacation; I could relax without the weight of my real life.

But less than two months later it was all gone.

★ ★ ★

In this book we are going to unpick the thoughts and behaviors around our possessions, steadily pulling on the thread and seeing what comes undone. Each chapter is themed around an object that I lost in the fire, and this becomes the jumping-off point for exploring a different lesson I have since learned about stuff.

We all have a relationship to our stuff that is both unique to us and similar to that of many others, so throughout the book we will hear both from researchers who can explain common behavioral patterns and from individuals who have a distinctive approach to owning things.

We will start by looking at how dopamine can cause us to feel a thrill when shopping. We'll look at how we can use stuff as a distraction, and how companies exploit this weakness to get us to buy their products.

Then we'll assess the role of status: why people splash cash on cars or use stuff in subtle ways to mark their place in society, and how having the right things can be a form of communication. We will look at why keeping up with the Joneses is not necessarily a silly thing to do but is in fact something bred into us for social cohesion and protection.

We will consider the role of clothes and other decorative items as forms of self-expression. We will look at how these can both help mark us out as individuals and allow us to fit in with the group.

After that, we will examine scarcity and how our minds go haywire when things are in short supply. We will look at how the idea of limited resources influences our buying behavior, whether it's toward diamonds or Coca-Cola.

Next we will look at how collecting affects the mind. By considering examples of healthy and unhealthy behaviors, we will see how collecting is about so much more than the things you buy.

We will then look at the ways in which memory works, and why our stuff can be so crucial for it. We will learn about how owning something for a long time warps our ability to judge its value, and the psychological effects that make it so hard to get rid of some of our oldest belongings. We will look at how to improve our memories without using stuff, before considering the effect of nostalgia on the mind. I hope that along the way you will be able to sift through some of your things, and the memories that go along with them, and see if there are any that you can let go of.

At this point we'll try to come up with a list of the things that we genuinely need. I will propose simple guidelines that can help us to properly recognize the difference between wants and needs, and show how advertising has led us to confuse the two.

As we get to the end, we'll think about another type of need: our desire for beautiful things. We will turn to philosophy and science to try to work out what beauty is, and why it's so important.

Finally, to end on a positive note, we will discover the science-backed ways that allow you to truly buy happiness. It's not a matter of shopping in the right places but of rethinking the role of money in our lives—and what it can really do.

Good luck.

Satisfaction Isn't Found While Shopping

I spent my early adulthood in a state of near-constant distraction.

In the morning, I would listen to the radio as I got ready, then put my earphones in the minute I left the house to walk to the station. When I sat down on the train, I paused the music while I read a book, then pressed play again as soon as I got to my stop. All day at work I was stressed and busy, then afterward I would turn on music for the journey to meet friends or on my wanderings around the shops. On the weekends I had five or six social plans, sometimes spending just an hour at one before going to the next. If I was doing laundry, I would do it with the TV on loud in the next room.

I felt restless nearly all the time. It was like I was always trying to be somewhere else, but I wasn't exactly sure where that was.

★ ★ ★

The urge for noise, stimulation, conversation, and distraction was strongest when I was at home alone. It felt like the air had been stripped of its usual padding—the boiling of a kettle or the closing of a drawer that showed there was another life in the house—and without it, my mind rattled around in the cold, hard silence.

It was always worse when I was feeling generally unhappy. If I had had a fight with my boyfriend before leaving for work in the morning, I would spend the day frantically texting friends to see if anyone was free for a drink that evening. If the clock turned six and I still had no plans, I would initiate my emergency backup: shopping. I would wander up and down Regent Street in London, stroking cashmere scarves and trying on dresses. I spent so many evenings there that I knew the shops' individual little routines—the way that the music was switched off ten minutes before they closed, or how after a certain time the doors would stop opening automatically and you had to ask an assistant to slide them open manually.

Sometimes I bought things, but not always. I was there primarily to have somewhere brightly lit and noisy to go for a few hours. I wanted to be surrounded by people; I wanted to look at some shiny, new things for a minute; I wanted to be distracted.

When I was alone at home I did something similar. I would watch television in brief glances when I looked up from my phone, where I would be scrolling through some shopping website or another. Often I would sit on my sofa, looking at other people's living rooms on social media—I was trying to work out what I needed to buy to make my home feel that welcoming.

One of those accounts pointed me toward an email subscription service that promised to send me highlights of shopping websites. In bored moments at work, or worried moments at home, I opened the emails, often clicking through to buy whatever it was they had recommended to me. I was on a low starting salary in journalism, but instead of that stopping me, I just turned to the cheapest items available.

I liked each thing individually but abhorred the overall impression it created. It felt ephemeral; the rose-gold plant pots had arrived yesterday and would be out of style by tomorrow. These things were visitors in my home, never permanent residents. I replaced the cheap fairy lights every year.

The impermanence of what I bought contrasted with the endurance of the hand-me-downs I'd been given. I had a warm brown 1960s coffee table from my grandparents that my dad could remember from his childhood. On top of it I put some hollow colored glass candle holders that I had seen on Instagram.

Sometimes we shop thinking about what will benefit us over the next few decades. At other times, all we consider is the next five minutes.

★ ★ ★

You have probably heard of dopamine, although what you have heard might not be accurate. The word is commonly used in the phrase "dopamine rush" to describe the pleasure people get from scrolling social media, for example, or eating junk food. That's not an entirely correct use of the term, as I learned in several conversations with Professor Ciara McCabe, a neuroscientist at the University of Reading in the United Kingdom who researches how the brain's dopamine system works.

Dopamine definitely does make you feel good, she says, and can even cause something as strong as euphoria. But it doesn't do this just whenever something good happens—it is in fact more closely linked to the anticipation of reward. That thrill, that jolt of pleasure you feel before doing something, is dopamine—you are anticipating how you will feel.

But dopamine does more than just make us feel good. It works on several circuits in the brain simultaneously, including networks that control learning and memory and those that control movement.

Professor McCabe explains why dopamine would have such far-reaching effects. She gives an example of one of our ancestors wandering across the landscape searching for food. When she unexpectedly stumbled across a tree full of fruit, she would have felt a rush of dopaminergic joy (we were much more easily pleased back then). But this joy is not particularly useful if it doesn't also get us to repeat our actions in future, and again find that tree full of fruit. In 2004, researchers in Seattle showed the importance of dopamine to learning by testing how well mice that were bred to be dopamine deficient could learn the escape route in a swimming task.[1] With low levels of dopamine, these mice showed "no evidence of learning" compared to the control group, meaning that they would struggle as much on their second or third attempt at the task as they did on their first. Despite trying it several times, they seemed to take little or nothing in. However, their learning ability seemed to improve when they were treated with L-dopa, an amino acid that is converted into dopamine in the body.

Just as dopamine helps us to learn, it also begins to shape our habits. If we have learned that a certain tree bears fruit, then we will habitually go there to check on it. If we have learned that our social media apps give us the satisfaction of invitations or sweet messages from friends, then we will routinely open them and scroll through. And if we know that, through internet shopping, we sometimes find clothes that fit perfectly, then we will browse our favorite sites in order to make ourselves feel good.

Over time, we stop thinking about these habits and how we've acquired them. Our brains also get used to the reward that they bring and stop releasing as much dopamine, meaning we enjoy the rewards less. We just carry on out of habit.

Katie Hart has a job title that sounds either very interesting or a little bit sinister. She is a neuromarketing specialist, meaning that she helps companies make convincing ads by looking at the effect they have on their customers' brains. Through the use of a brain-scanning headset and a pair of eye-tracking glasses, Hart can work out what our subconscious minds really think about a product.

One of the most common mistakes that marketers make is thinking that advertisements should appeal to our rational minds, she says. Simply telling customers that a product is objectively the best in one way or another—that it's the "biggest, quickest, or the cheapest"—doesn't work. To get their attention, you've got to make a customer feel something, says Hart.

The most effective way of doing this is to create an "emotional lift" by going on a journey through the ad, starting with a negative and ending with a positive. The negative opening grabs our attention by making us worried, then the positivity at the end feels like a reward for our minds, she says. If used correctly, these ads can make us want things we've never wanted before.

When Hart has someone strapped into a headset, there are six markers she is looking for in their brain that will help her to inform clients how well their ads are working. The first is excitement, a measure of general physical arousal that could be positive, like butterflies in the stomach, or negative, like feeling anxious. The second is engagement, or how much brainpower someone is expending in concentration. Next is focus, which is whether your attention is drifting around or stuck to one thing. Then it's relaxation—too much is not good, as it means an ad will go in one ear and out the other. The fifth metric is stress, which assesses how comfortable you feel watching something. And lastly, there is aversion: Is it thumbs up, or thumbs down?

Each client wants customers to feel different levels of these emotions depending on what they're selling, says Hart. A company selling bath bombs is probably looking for a low score on stress compared to a firm marketing boot camp fitness classes. But the brain activity shown on one of these scans is a brilliantly accurate predictor of whether or not we will eventually buy the product, says Hart, and much better than if you simply ask someone what they will do, which engages their rational, not emotional, brain.

But no matter how good the ad is, marketing can't make you want literally anything: The best it can do is make you want something that is on the periphery of an existing desire. For example, no ad will convince me to buy soccer cleats, but I could be steadily persuaded into considering a better tennis rackct (the one I have came from the lost and found box at my local community club).

★ ★ ★

The more you think about our desires for material possessions, the less they seem to make sense. Logically, getting what you want should satisfy you. If you've wanted a fancy set of pajamas for a while, then once you buy them your level of desire should cool down a little. But that doesn't always happen. When you have the satin pajamas you wanted, that desire can actually increase—once you feel the sheen against your skin, everything else starts to seem different. Your fleece slippers might have seemed comfortable before, but now they look worn; you used to love your cozy bed sheets, but now they look faded. If you're now the kind of person who looks chic even when sleeping, then those old things aren't good enough for you anymore. Buying the new thing was akin to climbing a hill—you are still looking at the same landscape but from a different point.

This is called the Diderot effect—the idea that buying one thing makes you want a whole load of other new things. It got its name from an eighteenth-century French philosopher called Denis Diderot, who wrote about the idea in an essay called "Regrets for my Old Dressing Gown, or A warning to those who have more taste than fortune." He writes about how his "old robe was one with the other rags that surrounded me," while with the new one "all is now discordant." He goes on to describe how the unleashing of dissatisfactions and desires that the new dressing gown brought sent him into a spiral of debt and caused him much stress.

Maybe you aren't a French philosopher and therefore can't imagine getting so emotional about a dressing gown that you ruin your life over it. But there is another version of the effect too: New things seem to require other things to go with them. If you buy a laptop, a whole range of new wants are opened up to you—laptop covers, an additional keypad, a stand to raise it to eye level. If you buy a new dress for your birthday, it's tempting to get the shoes and earrings to match.

Wanting is an emotion that attaches itself to the most convenient thing it can find. Once you've bought that new thing, the wanting will simply swing around and find something else to latch onto.

Something I find remarkable about our current shopping culture is how normal it seems when it is anything but. Every autumn I find myself having the same conversation with someone, where after commenting on the darker evenings or nippy mornings, they say that they need to buy clothes for the new season. Before the fire I would just nod my head in silent agreement, but more recently I've started to question that response.

The way we buy new things in the rich and modern world is deeply abnormal, and wildly different from how the vast majority of people who have ever existed have lived.

The United States, as it so often is, is a complete outlier, with people buying an average of fifty-three new pieces of clothing a year.[2] If everyone around you shops like that, if every time you see a character on a TV show they're wearing something new, if sales assistants always tell you to treat yourself, then it might seem normal. But even compared to similar countries this is very odd—in the United Kingdom, people on average buy thirty-three new pieces of clothing a year.[3]

We could also compare ourselves with people not from other places but from other times. To estimate the belongings that people had in the past, we can look at inventories taken after death for the purposes of a will. (It should be noted how different even this is from our current way of living—my clothes are mostly so crappy that no one would want to inherit them after I die, and yet are so numerous that making a list of them would be nearly impossible.)

An inventory of the belongings of Mary Cooley, a nurse-midwife from York County, Virginia, who died in 1778, has been recorded as part of the Colonial Williamsburg online library collection.[4] She owned ten gowns, six petticoats, thirteen aprons, fifteen caps, and nine shifts, perhaps with some other older clothing that was considered not worth listing.

And even Cooley owned a lot of clothes, if we compare her to people who lived earlier in history. In 1631, a widow was recorded as receiving a clothing allowance of "one pair of shoes and a chemise every two years and a dress of coarse cloth every three."[5]

I have a friend who treats shopping in a very strange way. She goes shopping at least once a week and gets parcel after parcel delivered to her door, but she keeps almost none of it. "I just love the thrill of buying something," she told me once. "It doesn't matter if I take it all back afterward; I still got that thrill of trying on something new."

She didn't need to learn about the science of dopamine—she instinctively knew that the biggest rush of shopping joy comes right at the beginning, when you rip open the package that's just been delivered. So shouldn't we all be acting like her, buying and returning things all the time, to get the thrill with none of the consequences?

Unfortunately, while it might not be immediately obvious, buying and returning stuff has a huge environmental cost. Even if we ignore the toll of actually manufacturing the things, the buying and returning itself has an impact. When you order online, the typical courier delivery emits 181 g of carbon dioxide per item for each journey,[6] which could be multiplied many times if, like me, you're never home when your parcels are delivered and they have to attempt the drop-off several times.

The bad news continues once the company has received your return. When you order clothes online, they always come perfectly folded, packed in sealed pouches, and smelling faintly of plastic. But when you return things, do you post them back in this condition? Of course not, and it would be impossible to, given that you had to rip the packets open to get to the clothes, which now smell of your perfume.

Sadly, that means that a lot of stock is simply discarded on return, as it is not in good enough condition to resell. Optoro, a reverse logistics company (i.e., it handles returns), estimates that 2.3 million tons of returns end up in landfills every year in the United States.[7] Recently, I spoke to an American woman who said that some US companies had gone a step further. She had recently ordered a blanket that wasn't right when it arrived. She asked the company for a return label, but they suggested something else. Instead of paying for extra shipping, processing, and disposal themselves, they got her to do it for them. They asked her to throw the blanket in her own garbage bin, then send them a picture. Her money was swiftly paid back.

Fleeing Boredom

Often, shopping can be a brief escape from boredom or a distraction from unpleasant feelings. We might not be desperately unhappy but simply feeling the beginning of the nagging sense of restlessness that comes when we spend too long without having fun.

In 2019 some Swedish researchers studied the phenomenon of how people impulse shop when they're bored.[8] Instead of doing a quantitative study by gathering data and analyzing it numerically, they collected qualitative information by interviewing young Swedes and asking open-ended questions about their shopping habits and feelings around it.

The participants said a lot of things which felt . . . relatable. "Boredom, I felt bored. I probably just felt that it would be fun with something new. It would improve my situation right now," said twenty-four-year-old Emelie. Several of them gave accounts of how they online shop, revealing their private habits in a way that feels confessional. A man called Niklas said that he often does it late at night, in that odd in-the-middle time between turning off the TV and going to bed. A woman called Ida also recalled late-night shopping, sitting at her mother's kitchen table alone at 1:30 a.m. Searching for something to entertain her, she opened her emails and found a voucher for a 40 percent discount on curtains. Some participants said that they spent up to three hours a day browsing shopping sites to relieve boredom.

The authors of the paper note that the participants spoke about how the emotions driving them made shopping feel like a "'must have' craving rather than a utility need." They were on the "hunt for joy," and the actual thing they bought at the end was just one of several rewards from the experience.

Some people are aware of this and are taking drastic steps to reduce their restless hunt. Sometime around 2018, the concept of dopamine fasting started taking off—the idea that by quitting things that usually bring immediate pleasure, you can reset your mind and reduce your addiction to stimulation. People tried different regimes, but the fasts usually involved avoiding the following: shopping, tasty food, sex, hugs, good conversation, alcohol, TV, social media, technology, and pornography. Some people were even more restrictive, stopping themselves from reading books they liked or from exercising, to make sure that they didn't get any post-workout thrills.

The aim was to reduce their brain's reliance on high levels of stimulation to feel sated so that afterward they would find normal tasks more pleasurable.

Plenty of people claim that this practice works: After a day of abstaining from excitement, they feel they have retrained their brain's response to dopamine and can find small things pleasurable again. Scientists aren't quite so sure that this is what is happening, pointing out that while you might be able to "fast" from food or sex, you can't fast from a naturally occurring chemical in your body any more than you can fast from breathing.[9] That doesn't necessarily mean that fasts don't work. Having a day of sitting around doing little, not working, not checking your emails, not doing hard exercise, not getting wasted, and not running from one social engagement to the next will probably feel good after a long week. It is called resting.

Patience

When we are shopping on impulse, it can be something like scratching an itch: We feel an urge and instantly satisfy it. It's like the feeling of craving something salty, or opening up a social media app on your phone without thinking about it. Over time, the dopamine we receive from these pleasures has taught us to associate certain triggers with rewards and has shaped our behavior as a result—so we open the app as soon as we see its logo, or eat a handful of chips as soon as we see the bowl at a party. The trigger could even be an emotional one.

We have come to learn that because the itchiness briefly disappears when we take particular actions, it is these actions that are the solution. If we were to run a scientific experiment to test this theory, we would need to set up a control for comparison—to see what happens to the urge if we do nothing and simply wait.

Versions of this experiment are suggested by personal finance experts. Some recommend simple solutions to wanting: When you feel the urge to buy, just note down what you want and return to it seventy-two hours later. If you still want it then, you can buy it—guilt-free. Others suggest longer waits, sometimes of up to thirty days, in order to truly test the strength and verity of your desires, but in my experience wants are so fleeting that seventy-two hours is usually more than enough time.

I tested the waiting strategy myself before going into a full "no-buy month" as described later on in the book. The effects were humbling. Every time I walked down the street and saw a woman in a nicer coat than mine, or scrolled past some piece of fitness equipment that I wanted, I just wrote down what it was on a note in my phone. Not only had my desires faded three days later, but most of the time I had completely forgotten about them. I discovered the note on my phone while writing a shopping list a few months later. "Coat but nice" and "thing for abs"—I couldn't even remember what that meant.

★ ★ ★

What strikes me when thinking about our cravings for stuff is the restlessness of it: We think that what we have is not enough, and we can't stop thrashing around trying to do something about it. Maybe the urge isn't entirely wrong—we might truly lack something—but the promised answer of new stuff will not help but instead may lead us into a state of jittery need, action, and disappointment. Like the aphorism says, we keep repeating the same action hoping for a different result. We have gone mad.

I've done this more than anyone. Buying, and even just browsing, has been a welcome distraction in the most distressing periods of my life. Not only can it occupy my mind for a few minutes, but it also gives me a simple explanation for my unhappiness: *It is not a sign that something is drastically wrong with my mind or my life—it's just that I don't have the right pair of boots yet.*

This is unhelpful for a few reasons. Firstly, it's just wrong. Buying something will not extinguish your yearning—it will soon return attached to something else. This searching and buying positions happiness as something that is always just slightly out of our reach. We postpone happiness for a tomorrow that never comes, all the while distracting ourselves from what could make us feel truly better.

FINAL THOUGHTS

CONSIDER THE DIDEROT EFFECT

As we learned earlier, the Diderot effect occurs when having one new thing makes us want more. Just like the example of the dressing gown, one shiny brand-new item can make the rest of our possessions look shabby in contrast.

Try to guard against this where you can. After you have been shopping, be mindful of how you feel afterward when putting things away. Do you suddenly get ideas of other things to buy? If so, perhaps try the noting exercise below.

WRITE DOWN WHAT YOU WANT

When I was a teenager, I used to write down the things I wanted to buy in pocket-sized notebooks. My desires were much bigger than my pocket money, so any time I wanted to buy something, I simply noted it down with the date in the book, hoping that some of these desires could later be satisfied at Christmas. When I go back to my parents' house, I sometimes leaf through these little notebooks and laugh. An entry from 2006 cries out for boot-cut jeans "with jewels on." In 2010, I was lusting after a "scarf, very large."

I didn't realize it then, but these notebooks were very helpful. Over time they gave me a budding sensation that not every momentary urge has to be satisfied, as most will pass of their own accord. After the 2006 entry, I never again wrote about wanting bejeweled jeans.

If you are someone who finds themselves wanting a lot of things on a whim, I recommend that you give writing them down a go. In some ways, it can itself help to scratch the itch. Part of the urge to buy can come from the worry that unless you do it straight away, you'll forget the brilliant idea you've just had. Record it now, thank your mind for suggesting it, and come back to it later.

WAIT

If you want to go further, try out a waiting period before buying. You could go for the thirty-day wait, or even just a seventy-two-hour one. After a cooling-off period, it is much easier to tell the difference between what you actually want and what was simply a passing urge.

PACK AWAY YOUR THINGS

A few years ago I divided my clothes in two, between things I wear in winter and those I wear in summer. There is some crossover (in the United Kingdom, you need to have a cardigan on hand all year round), but many things are season-specific—you never need shorts in December or a Christmas sweater in July.

I bought some vacuum seal storage bags, and every April and September I put one season's clothes away in the bottom of my wardrobe and bring out the other's. Each time I take out the "new" things, they feel exciting and fresh again after time apart, and they mark the beginning of a new season. I have effectively tricked myself into seeing old things as new, making me want what I already have.

REDUCE TRIGGERS

Our appetite for new things is frivolous and easily led. You can use this to your advantage by reducing the number of triggers that lead you to want them. Perhaps it would help to unfollow a specific person on social media who is always showing off their new clothes. When I'm on my lunch-break walk, I follow a route that goes through the park instead of through a shopping center. Removing the opportunity to "just have a look" in a shop dramatically reduces the quantity of things that I want.

You Are More Than Your Things

One Christmas I found a huge box waiting for me under the tree. It contained a pecan-brown leather jewelry box, about a foot high, with four slim drawers lined with cream velvet. The lid flipped open to reveal a mirror and fastened shut with a polished brass lock.

I pushed aside some of the perennial mess that lived on top of my chest of drawers to make a space for the box, where it looked completely out of place: a perfect, neat object looming over the thickets of clutter. In those slender drawers I laid a few pairs of silver earrings and a string of pearls I'd been given for my sixteenth birthday.

The things in there couldn't have been worth more than a few hundred dollars, but they were incredibly special to me. These were the most valuable things I owned, items that I brought out on special occasions only, to look my absolute best at parties or weddings.

I imagined owning the jewelry box for decades into the future, keeping my shards of glitter safely locked away until I needed their sparkle. I thought about blowing the dust off the top as I got ready for a Christmas party, or opening the box on my wedding day and clipping the pearls around my neck, taking on the luster of expensive things.

★ ★ ★

We were in a dark bar in east London on a Saturday night, sitting on backless stools. The table was low to the ground, which I didn't like because it meant I had nowhere to hide. The walls were covered with fake plastic foliage, the cocktail menu resisted being unpeeled from the table. The music was loud, so while my then-boyfriend, Joel, leaned back against the wall, I leaned forward to hear.

"I like girls who dress right," he said, and I nodded, pretending to understand what that meant. "You know, the ones who don't try hard to look good—they just wake up and put on some boxy shirt."

Around our feet were half a dozen shopping bags. We'd spent the afternoon shopping on London's smartest streets, him leading the way with confidence while I tagged behind. His card was linked to his parents' account, and he spent with the carefree abandon of someone who has seen that the weather forecast predicts no rainy days ahead. He piled up so many bags that I had to help carry a few, looping the ribbon handles over my forearms. From time to time, I caught sight of us in a shop window. In the glass's darkened image, we were two young people charging forward into life, the bags on our arms leading the way. We looked like we belonged together.

We went back to his house. He tossed his new coat on a chair and put on music that I didn't recognize. On the table he kept a pile of art-house fashion magazines, their spines uncracked. The women on the covers all looked the same: tall, very thin, their lips parted but no sound coming out.

The next morning he woke me up and told me I had to go home. He had people coming over and wanted time to get things ready. It was clear that I was not invited.

When I got home, I looked around my bedroom with new eyes. What had been my refuge the day before now seemed hideously embarrassing. I despaired at the flowery cushion covers, averted my eyes from the velvet lampshade, and cringed at the photos of friends I'd stuck onto my wardrobe. The earnestness of it, the unsophistication, the childishness: It all felt mortifying compared to the vision of urbane adulthood that I'd now seen. I had to change.

★ ★ ★

To become a nun, you must promise to follow three rules. There is obedience, following the orders of your superiors; and then chastity, which is self-explanatory. Finally, there is poverty, where you pledge to give up all personal possessions. You will have all the food, shelter, and clothes you need provided, but nothing will belong to you personally. Everything is shared.

It was this principle of poverty that most attracted Sister Monica Williams when she came to the sisterhood in 1970. "The idea of sharing goods was quite instrumental in my coming to community," she says. "I wanted to not have anything of my own." She hoped that a community where no one owned things would lead to perfect equality, with no one-upping each other with new fashions or styles.

She is now in her seventies but seems young in many ways, with hair as red as an autumn leaf and the sort of disciplined faith in her beliefs that usually burns off after adolescence. She didn't come from a wealthy family, but what she owned growing up was very different than what she had after joining the convent in her early twenties.

In fact, she owns so few things that I can list the entirety of them here:

- Eyeglasses
- Some underwear
- A pen
- A toothbrush
- A pair of shoes
- A box of family photographs
- Four habits (two for summer and two for winter)
- An outfit of "civilian" clothes she wears when visiting family

Everything else she uses, from the mugs she drinks from to the bed she sleeps in, is effectively loaned to her.

She keeps her things in her room, which has simple furniture owned by the convent. Sister Monica says that new nuns are often shocked by the fact that their rooms don't have wardrobes. Nuns own so little that they don't need them: A spare habit can be hung on a peg on the door, and underwear is kept in a small set of drawers.

Sister Monica's life shows us that life is profoundly different without stuff. There's no cachet to wearing a habit from one shop or another, no way of showing how well you keep up with the trends.

Over the decades since becoming a nun, Sister Monica has decided that "poverty" is not the right way to describe a life without stuff. To her, poverty is going without your basic needs in life: clothes, shelter, food. She has all those things. The twenty or so sisters live in a converted former care home in Yorkshire, northern England. The house is clean and tidy, with white walls and a room set aside downstairs as a chapel.

She is never worried about paying the mortgage; she never chases invoices; she never has to fret about the gas bill. "I am in no way financially poor," she says. "People think we live poorly . . . but compared to most people, we don't." Instead, her community is "rich, because we . . . care for each other."

Showing Off Our Status with Stuff

According to traditional economic theory, humans make only rational decisions when they are shopping. If someone sees a skirt she likes, she should be much happier to pay twenty dollars for it than two hundred.

But sometimes we do the exact opposite: When something has a high price, we want to buy it even more. These items are called Veblen goods, after Thorstein Veblen, a nineteenth-century American economist who wrote about how we use our stuff to gain social status. In his 1899 book, *The Theory of the Leisure Class*, Veblen examines the shopping habits of the American upper classes, including their taste for showy and expensive stuff bought to demonstrate their wealth.

> [Flowers] that can be cultivated with relative ease are accepted and admired by the lower middle class ... [but] are rejected as vulgar by those people who are better able to pay for expensive flowers ... while still other flowers, of no greater intrinsic beauty than these, are cultivated at great cost and call out much admiration....

In other words, Veblen says that sometimes we buy expensive stuff simply because it's expensive—we associate rich people with high status, so we buy expensive things in the hope they will lend us social status. A lot has changed since then, but Veblen's original example holds true: Fashionable florists work with expensive peonies and orchids, and ignore cheaper carnations.

There are plenty of other examples of this effect. Imagine two trench coats: one from a luxury brand, and the second identical to it in every way except for the label. Would you pay the same price for each? Of course not; no one would. When you buy the luxury coat, you are not only paying for a functional item that keeps you warm and dry, you are also paying for the social status that it brings.

Professor Jill Sundie of Washington and Lee University in Virginia is something of a modern successor to Veblen. She has put forward a set of principles that determine what becomes a status symbol and what doesn't. According to her research, it boils down to three things: wastefulness, rarity, and observability. Beyond those three criteria, Sundie says that what becomes a status symbol is pretty arbitrary.

Wastefulness

The first element, wastefulness, refers to the excessive use of money, effort, time, or other resources used to obtain an item. It's a subtle marker of your economic status: Showing that you don't have to cut corners in your choice of coat demonstrates that you have money to spare.

Wastefulness looks very different in different cultures. When we talk, Sundie tells me about the Abelam people of Papua New Guinea, an agrarian society that lives in the rainforest. "They compete for social status by growing yams: If you can grow the biggest yam that's so big and tough it's not even edible any more, then that's the route to status in that society," she says. I encourage you to look up pictures of these yams, which are completely unlike anything you would see in the supermarket. The longest yams look like tree trunks, require several men to carry them, and, according to Sundie, are so woody and fibrous that they are completely inedible. Once they've been dug up, they are decorated and paraded around in displays instead of being eaten.

For people outside that culture, this might sound a little odd: a perfect example of how silly it is to spend time, money, and effort producing things just to show off. But it doesn't look that way to Sundie, who compares the yams to expensive cars. Small yams are cheaper to produce (and tastier) than enormous ones, just like a Peugeot is much cheaper than a Ferrari. You might add that these are totally different things—but no amount of money spent on a car will make you go faster through traffic. "The fact that you can waste your resources on something that doesn't have any functional benefits indicates that you have resources to burn," she says.

Once I had heard this rule, I saw it everywhere. I thought about a brief stint I'd had in a corporate office before I became a journalist, where I remember my boss leaning forward to point something out on my screen. As she did so, the label of her dress poked out. Her quietly elegant black dress hadn't looked like anything special, but the label told another story: It was Dolce & Gabbana! I couldn't imagine how much it had cost, but certainly many times more than the pencil skirt I was wearing, which I'd gotten from a supermarket. Spending that extra money in such a subtle way felt like a true power move to me. She didn't need to shop around to find the cheapest options; she could afford to be wasteful with her money.

Similar behavior was examined in a South Korean paper from 2020. It looked at how giving luxury items a "functional use" was a covert but powerful status symbol, or, as the title snappily put it, "Your dream is my reality." Across a range of tests, they found that people had respect not just for those who bought luxury goods, but especially so for those who used those goods in a casual manner. If you have a Louis Vuitton handbag that you keep in its dustcover and bring out on special occasions, you'll gain a certain amount of social status. But you'll get much more if you're using it to lug your gym kit around, letting your water bottle leak into the lining.

Rarity

Sundie says that something can only be a status symbol if it is rare—a giant yam or a sports car won't give you social status if everyone has one. Rarity is also an indirect marker that something is difficult to acquire, and signals that its owner has a skill or resource that not everyone has.

A good example of this is the Birkin handbag, made by the French luxury brand Hermès. To the untrained eye, these are nothing out of the ordinary: They are almost square in shape, with two short handles and a metal buckle that you twist to close. But since their release in 1984, they have become a status symbol of the highest order. Owning one simultaneously demonstrates your financial prowess (at the time of writing, there is a secondhand Birkin listed for around $335,000 on a fashion resale site) and your social know-how (only the most connected people are permitted to buy one new).

The byzantine procedure for acquiring a Birkin bag is examined on a 2015 episode of the NPR podcast *Planet Money*, on which two people describe their odysseys.[1] One man was told at multiple Hermès branches that they were sold out and was offered a place on the waiting list—which meant a wait of up to four years. At one store he was told that even the waiting list was full, but he could have a slot on the waiting list for the waiting list. Another woman interviewed for the show had similar difficulties: Although she had the $60,000 or so needed to buy one, no store she visited would even show her a bag. She resorted to asking the mother of a friend, who had previously bought one, to set up an introduction between her and the brand in the hope that a personal recommendation would help.

The hosts asked a marketing expert about Hermès's explanation that the supply of Birkins is limited because they take a lot of effort to produce. He said it was nonsense, and that their exclusivity was actually a smart advertising strategy, one that had driven the social cachet of the bags through the roof. "They play hard to get. That's how they seduce you," he said. "It creates a bond once you're in. It makes you feel that you're worthy."

Observability

The final element of the status symbol as identified by Sundie is observability: Other people must be able to see the item, although this "audience" doesn't need to be huge. It could range from the one person who sees your luxury pajamas at night to the hundreds or thousands of people following you on social media.

Your audience can be specific, too, depending on who you want to impress. If you live by the beach, maybe a boat is an important status symbol, while in the city it might be a bespoke suit.

Status symbols also vary between socioeconomic groups, with the gap growing wider over the past few decades. Since the flashy 1980s, sociologists have noticed that the upper classes are moving away from spending their spare cash on physical objects and are instead putting money toward less visible forms of status, like travel, private education, and memberships to boutique gyms.

Research by Professor Elizabeth Currid-Halkett, an expert in the consumer economy, shows that Americans in the top income bracket spent an average of at least $20,400 a year on education in 2014 (the most recent year that figures are available).[2] But those with middle-class incomes spent between $400 and $600 a year: a huge discrepancy, and one that is growing over time.

Part of this shift to spending on "self-improvement" through health and education could be read as a desire to gain social status by demonstrating that you have more than just money. Rich people want to show that they have taste and education too. An example of this might be the industry of "book curators" who fill the bookshelves of the rich and famous. In the United States, the best known is the Colorado-based Thatcher Wine, who purchases books on behalf of wealthy clients, often wrapping them in customized paper covers to make them look prettier on the shelf.

Among his clients is Gwyneth Paltrow, who commissioned Wine to buy and style "five or six hundred books" to fill the empty shelves of her Los Angeles house. Instead of gradually expanding her collection of books over time as she read them, Paltrow, as Wine told an American magazine, asked for titles in a "rigid color palette of black, white and gray."[3]

To see what it's about, I visited Ultimate Library, a book curator in Chelsea, a prestigious neighborhood of southwest London. Their office is one long room, with the desks gathered together in a corner, shrinking away from the masses of books that cover every other inch of space.

The company's orders range from small to large, from putting together a shelf of ten books about boats for a superyacht to four thousand books for a feature display in a high-end restaurant. Their typical private client falls somewhere in the middle: They have a (first, second, fifth) home with a large study or library, and they want tasteful books to cover the bare shelves.

Over the years, the company has developed a way of putting together their libraries. First, they pull together a skeleton of books on whatever topics you're interested in—say, yoga or history. Then they add flesh, starting with a layer of secondhand books for "texture"—to make the library look like it's developed organically over time—as well as a mix of recent, buzzy releases to show that you keep on top of trends. Some clients have specific aesthetic desires too: books in particular colors, ones bound in leather or in fancy cloth covers.

Simonne Waud, a senior member of staff, tells me about a large job they did recently for the huge games room of a villa in the chic Notting Hill area of west London. They filled the lower shelves—the ones that you could see and reach—with "more contemporary and more intelligent books." But they filled the top shelves, where the books were too high to pull down and read and too far away for anyone to see the titles, with "filler books just to create that look."

On the surface, the idea seems strange: Why would people install so many bookshelves if they don't have enough books to fill them? And couldn't you just fill the shelves with trinkets, photos, or something else? Waud explains that there is something particular about displaying a curated collection of books: It "reflects them." It shows the world who they are, or who they hope to be.

Why Do We Crave Status?

Now that we know about the elements of a status symbol, let's consider *why we crave them in the first place*. Why do humans feel an urge for high social standing, and to demonstrate it via their stuff?

Scientists have been considering this question for hundreds of years. In 1860, Charles Darwin lamented that "the sight of a feather in a peacock's tail . . . makes me sick."[4] His theory of evolution stated that over time species become better suited to their environments, developing features that help them to survive. But Darwin couldn't understand why peacocks had evolved their long and, frankly, silly tail—what on earth would be the survival benefit of that? This is especially true given that such a tail could even be disadvantageous: Maintaining it requires extra energy from food and slows the peacock down when running away from a predator.

The reason is that looks matter: Peahens choose which peacock to mate with based on the size and shape of their tails. Just as the over-the-top nature of the yam contests or Birkin bags shows that their owners have so many resources that they can afford to be wasteful, so the peacock's shining tail demonstrates that it is in fine fettle and has ample food. Peahens interpret this as a good thing—their offspring will have the best possible chance of surviving.

Humans have more complex social networks, which means that how we appear to others is important not just for appealing to mates but also for forging relationships with our peers that will help us survive and thrive. We want other people to know the great things that we bring to the table—the financial resources, social connections, or knowledge—in the hope that they might want to help us and share what they have in return. And when we're trying to form these critical relationships, our stuff can be a useful way to communicate and form bonds with others, says Sundie. "It's how to make yourself attractive, not just for a mating relationship, but in a broader sense, for alliance partners," she says. "[It could be] finding people who will help my kids with math . . . [The question is]: How do I become somebody that people want to connect with?"

While exploring the topic of status, I kept bumping into two conflicting ideas: We are hardwired to seek and display social status, but equally, this pursuit brings us a lot of stress. We are striving to be at the top of the pile, believing that the resultant happiness will compensate for the stress of getting there.

But most of us are at the bottom or in the middle looking upward, which can be a very distressing experience, as multiple studies show. In 2014, researchers measured this by looking at the Tsimané people of Bolivia, finding that the men who weren't respected by their peers in village meetings had chemical differences compared to those who were.[5] Their urine had higher levels of the stress hormone cortisol, and they were at greater risk of respiratory infections, a major cause of death in their society.

At the beginning of this chapter, Sister Monica described the peace of her status-free life, and how, despite the challenges of following religious orders, joining a convent allows you to opt out of many of the worries of ordinary life.

The status-free ideals of a nun might sound extreme, but millions of people across the world have lived through a version of it. In the United Kingdom, whether your school was private or run by the state, in the north or south, almost all of us started each school day by pulling on a scratchy, dull-colored sweater and a matching skirt or trousers. I spent most of my days from ages four to sixteen in almost exactly the same outfit: a wool skirt with matching wool sweater. Just like Sister Monica, I found there was something relaxing about this ritual.

The opposite happened in the final two years of school, when you could wear what you liked. Instead of setting my alarm for 6:50 a.m. every morning, I now cranked it back to 6:30 so I had extra time to decide what to wear. The rules set by the school were minimal—no sheer clothing, no flip-flops, no pajamas—and left everything else up to us. When I got dressed each morning, my aim was to look cool but not like a try-hard, smart but not geeky, individual but not kooky. And to accomplish this with the limited money I earned from waitressing at the weekends.

Despite our newfound freedom, it took only a few weeks for my classmates and I to talk longingly of the years we'd spent in uniforms. The stress of demonstrating our status through our clothes was literally costing us sleep in the mornings and taking mental energy from the key task in hand, which was passing our exams. We were far from the only ones who thought that way. Two-thirds of British parents polled in 2017 supported uniform policies, despite it costing them an additional £213 (about $277) a year.[6]

The Tragedy of Status

An emerging body of evidence suggests that although our efforts to build status with possessions or money can work, it won't be in the way we might think. And the status we build from stuff and money is not the type that will bring lasting happiness.

Professor Cameron Anderson of the University of California, Berkeley, says that we should be careful to distinguish between two types of status: socioeconomic and sociometric. The former describes your position in society at large and is determined by a number of things, including how rich you are, your education level, and your profession. Sociometric status, on the other hand, describes the respect and admiration that you get within smaller groups such as your colleagues or friends.

It's true that your possessions are linked to your perceived socioeconomic status, particularly when you are being judged by people who don't know you well. In general, when we meet someone for the first time, we accord more social status to those we suspect have a lot of money and expensive things. This might feel important, but Anderson's research shows that gaining the good opinion of strangers is not the most effective way of boosting your happiness and well-being.

On the other hand, your sociometric status, or your standing among the people you actually know, has a very strong effect on how you feel. Anderson and collaborators coined the term "local-ladder effect" in a 2012 paper to describe how this feels: If you picture your friendship group or your team at work as a ladder, what rung are you on?[7] It turns out that if you think you're on the bottom rung, meaning the people around you don't respect you much, then your well-being will be lowered. This is probably not a surprise.

But what is surprising is that your sociometric status has a much stronger impact on your happiness than your socioeconomic status. If you earn a lot of money as a corporate lawyer but your colleagues don't respect how well you do your job, then you may not be as happy as someone who earns an average salary but is seen as a pillar of the community.

And unlike your social status with strangers, you can't build sociometric status with the stuff you own. Your friends will not like you more if you have a Rolex. Your neighbors won't necessarily invite you for dinner if you have a fancy car parked outside your house.

There are other ways to build this kind of status, and most of them are free. Being nice helps, as do generosity and loyalty.

Being intelligent works, too, as it shows that you might be a useful person to have around. Confident people also tend to be more valued by their peers, as people assume that those who act like they know what's going on actually do.

Having particular skills or talents is good, and these can be specific to the group that you're in, says Anderson. For example, if you're in a running group, being fast will help you to build status, and much more so than owning the most expensive trainers on the market. Anderson says that there is even a version of this within the community of academics who study social status: The pecking order is based on the number of times your papers are cited by other academics, with the most "influential" authors at the top. (The irony is not lost on him.)

We want social status, so we buy stuff to impress others. But it turns out that the only people who are impressed by stuff are strangers, and it's not their opinions that matter most to us. We often don't realize there is a much cheaper, and more effective, way to scratch this itch.

An Equal Life

So, is it worth it? To eschew status, become true equals, and live without things? Let's return to Sister Monica, the nun we spoke to at the start of the chapter, who knows more than most about what a life without status symbols is really like.

I asked her if she ever regrets committing her life to the sisterhood, and she replies with a certain and immediate no. But over the decades she has learned that there are a few downsides when you own nothing. To start with, when people don't own something themselves, when they can't proudly tell people that it's theirs, they tend not to take very good care of it—even when they are as morally upright as nuns.

Before she died, Sister Monica's mother used to make regular visits to see her daughter in the convent. She generally enjoyed herself but once took Sister Monica aside to make a plea: When she died, her daughter must sell or give away her furniture, instead of donating it to the convent. "She said: 'Because people here just put their cups down [on the tables with no coaster] and I don't want my furniture ruined!'" laughs Sister Monica. "It's not precious to you as an item, and you may not care for it as much as you would if that item was yours personally."

There's another potential setback to consuming things and resources very carefully, says Sister Monica. Owning nothing, and having no children, means she has trodden very lightly on the earth, and sometimes Sister Monica worries that when she dies, there will be little left behind to show that she lived. She doesn't own a home that could be a solid reminder of her life's work; she won't be able to pass on heirlooms to her children. Her personal belongings could be quickly packed up into a few boxes and redistributed among the nuns.

"I don't regret [becoming a nun]. But I'm thinking to myself: 'Wouldn't it be lovely to have grandchildren?" she says. "I've not left any legacy."

★ ★ ★

When I was younger, I would sometimes hang out with a girl who would quietly mutter judgy comments about people we walked past on the street. She would talk about everyone—girls our age who were still wearing skinny jeans, older women whose roots were showing, middle-aged men driving flashy cars to make them feel young. Eventually we stopped seeing each other, and it was partly because of this habit of hers. Whenever I said goodbye to her, I felt slightly on edge, wondering what snide things she was saying about me to others.

You will not be surprised to learn that she struggled with her self-esteem. She spent a lot of her free time browsing the social media of women who had been on reality TV, or who modeled, or did a combination of the two. She spent hours each day looking at these women, who counted strict diets and cosmetic surgery as part of their job, zooming in to see the tags on their handbags or to check the sizes of their waists. It all felt so sad.

It's simple to say: "Don't care what other people think!" It's a nice idea, but it's impractical. Of course we care about what other people think; it is impossible not to. And of course social status is important. It is so important that someone showing us disrespect can make us furious, while feeling that we aren't loved makes us miserable.

Hopefully by learning more about how social status works we can let go of some of this petty judginess that we mistake for true social status. Research confirms what you already know to be true: that your character is far more important. Being smart, generous, confident, loyal, or kind gains you respect. Unkindness does not. It turns out that no one is friends with you because of your handbag, or watch, or yams.

FINAL THOUGHTS

WHAT DO YOU NOTICE?

Given that we're hardwired to pay attention to status, we notice markers of it everywhere. Think about the things you immediately notice other people having, or the things that you would go home and mention to a partner or friend. Personally, I'm obsessed with fancy kitchens, and spend far too much of my free time browsing for ones that I will never be able to afford. Embarrassingly often, I go to someone's house and can name the exact make and range of their cabinets.

Perhaps you are not interested in kitchens at all, but instead you notice someone's car or watch or shoes, things that completely pass me by. Whatever it is, consider it in terms of the elements that we looked at above: wastefulness, rarity, and observability. Scratching the surface, even just a little bit, can help the scales to fall from your eyes. These things often have no inherent benefits over other things—they are arbitrary items that we have applied a range of other meanings to.

WHAT DO YOU ENVY?

Similarly, consider a thing that you notice other people have that you really want for yourself. Ask yourself the reasons why you want it: Is there some fundamental property of the item that sets it above others? Would you be willing to pay the same price for the item if it was the same in every way except for the brand?

PRICE IN CONTEXT

Take yourself out to browse in a variety of shops where things are priced differently. Try on a couple of things, and notice how you feel about the price of each item. How does this shift when you are in a high-end store compared to somewhere less expensive? Notice the tendency for something to seem to be worth more when it's surrounded by other pricey items, and vice versa. This is not a reflection of how much something is worth but is simply the false sheen of the brand.

Plentiful Things Aren't Worthless

After the fire happened, people kept asking me what I missed the most. They often assumed it would be a big-ticket item: furniture, jewelry, kitchen appliances. It sounded like a joke when I said that actually, one of the things that had really stumped me was that I had lost this great box of hair ties that were just absolutely, completely up to the job. They laughed, thinking I was using something trivial to deflect from how cut up I was feeling inside.

We assume that because something is cheap, or because it is plentiful, then its value is null. Some cheap things are worthless, and some expensive things are very valuable. But we should not extrapolate further.

Someone who has never jumped to that conclusion is my granny. Everything is precious to her. In her kitchen she keeps a stash of lightly used teabags in case she wants a second cup. Fish skins are kept to feed the dogs. Rips are stitched, clothes are preserved, things are used over and over again.

I went to see her recently and she told me about how she came to be so careful with the things she uses. When she was a little younger than I am now, she lived in Cardiff with my late granddad, my dad, and my aunty. They were on a strict budget, feeding four people on one salary while saving to buy a house. As a result, they owned three teaspoons. Not six, not four: just three. It was all they could afford, explained Granny. She rummaged in a dresser and brought them out. They were still in perfect condition, with barely a scratch on them fifty-five years after they were bought. It makes sense. If you could only afford three teaspoons, you would look after them.

But her postwar carefulness is at odds with the world today. In the early 1960s she could only afford three teaspoons, but, at the time of writing, you can buy four teaspoons for $3.16 at the supermarket.

In her dresser there are plenty of other things, too, including half a dozen sets of crockery. There are delicate black-and-white coffee cups, chunky blue pottery, and a beautiful brightly painted tea set, which belonged to her mother and must be the best part of a century old. Granny and her sisters jokingly called them "Uncle Cyril's dishes" because they only came out when he was visiting. She only rarely uses these sets now, and there is at least one that she has never used at all.

These sets were total luxuries, representing months of scrimping and saving. Since then, even more effort has gone into preserving them, keeping them in near-pristine condition, to make them last a very long time.

In fact, she looks after everything in that way. If you were to give her a department store cardigan, she could still be wearing it, with a few hand-stitched repairs, twenty years later.

When you have experienced scarcity, it is very difficult to change your mindset. Whatever you give my granny will be valued, as she has developed an ability to see how something could be useful in a pinch—not surprising, given that she's been in a few pinches before. Her resourcefulness and dedication make me feel abashed. I bought a set of six teaspoons two years ago, but somehow I now only have five. I have no idea what happened to the sixth.

★ ★ ★

A few days after the fire, I was beginning to get tired of feeling low. My eyelids were so swollen from crying, and I was getting tetchy from sitting inside too long. I wanted to leave the house, go for a run, and let some of the sadness inside me out. I have long hair that reaches to the middle of my back, so after putting on my running gear I went to get one of the hair ties lingering at the bottom of my handbag. But there was nothing there.

I went to find the big box of hair ties that had been on my bedside table before I moved. It was a clear plastic box of five hundred neon-bright hair ties: so many of them that I used them like water. I would forget a few at the gym, lend some to friends, leave a couple on my desk at work. However many I lost, there were always more left in the box.

And so I looked for the box, but I could not find it anywhere. It was not in my suitcase nor put away in the bathroom—I realized that it must have been in the fire.

I stomped my foot like a grounded teenager, so irritated that the one thing that stood between me and my ability to get out into the sunshine and feel better was a thin piece of elastic. I had taken them for granted because they were everywhere, but, as soon as they weren't, the value of a hair tie became very, very clear. I went to buy another box of them later in the day, by which point the light had faded and it was too dark to go out. As I scanned and paid, I thought about other things that we take for granted. We might use a plastic shopping bag only once, when it could last for years. We pack for vacation and forget our sandals, so we pick up cheap flip-flops and, when they don't fit in our suitcase, we just leave them behind in the hotel room.

But this is all such a new thing. We used to wash and reuse tin foil, or open Christmas presents with scissors so that the wrapping paper could be used again. So why do we now treat some of the most useful things as if they're worthless?

★ ★ ★

Inside that question, there is another one hiding. Are rare things always so special?

One day, I was sent out on a story by the newspaper I worked for. I was to look around a new bank vault that had opened to serve London's billionaires.

I was greeted in the wood-paneled reception by a woman with a shiny blowout and even shinier black stilettos. Before showing me around, she gave me a security briefing, explaining the extensive lengths they went to in order to prevent break-ins. There were cameras, scanners, and sensors, but all were cleverly hidden, making the space feel like a luxury hotel—with fresh flowers at reception, grand stone fireplaces, and a patterned ceiling.

The woman led me around, showing me what they offered. The smallest spaces they had were safety deposit boxes the size of mailboxes, big enough to store passports, documents, or a necklace or two. The largest were entire rooms, which some people set up with racks to hang clothes, others filling them with antiques. Some people paid thousands of pounds a month to store their things there, but it was worth it, the woman explained. If you owned a collectible watch—one of only five ever produced—would you really run the risk of wearing it? Obviously not.

I nodded, not sure what to say.

It struck me that the vaults were in some ways a very fancy version of the storage unit I had rented, but for storing eighteenth-century marble consoles rather than pine kitchen tables. And because these people's things were so rare, they were more valued—in every sense of the word.

★ ★ ★

That night, I came home and opened my wardrobe to put my clothes away. The cardboard box marked "RANDOM" was there, as ever. Nothing about the box was special, really, except for the fact that it was the only one I had left, and because of its rarity, I had treated it well. Whenever I opened the wardrobe, I slowly ran my hand over the top of the box, removing any dust. A corner had been dented while moving, but I had pushed the cardboard in and down, back to where it should have been.

And while it wasn't in a vault, it somehow felt protected behind the wardrobe doors.

It had been months, and I still hadn't opened it. A few times, I had picked it up and shaken it to see if I could guess what was inside, like a child with a Christmas present. It was difficult to make out, but there was a dry shuffling noise that could have been paper, as well as the occasional thunk of something hard hitting the side. I was deeply, deeply curious about what was inside, yet I had never opened it up to see.

That evening, as I opened the wardrobe, I once again leaned down and pushed the dust off the top of the box, then ran a fingernail along the tape sealing it, creating a neat channel between the two sides on top. I could open it now; I could count the last fragments of the past. But I knew that, once again, I wouldn't.

The morning at the vault had rattled me a little. I wished I had been able to afford something like that; I wished my things had been kept that safe. The best I could do now was take good care of what I had left.

In the first few months, I hadn't opened the box because I was trying to avoid any sadness that would come with finding out exactly what I had lost: something I imagined as an irreversible finish, like a title card from an old film reading "The End." Over the months, my resolve to keep the box closed and the question open had only hardened.

Perhaps those safety deposit boxes stored priceless jewelry I could never dream of owning. But that was it; that was all they contained. A definite, finite parcel of stuff.

On one level, what I had was less than that: so limited that it fit into just one box. But my situation wasn't just constrained; paradoxically, it was infinite too. The possible contents of that box were endless. Keeping the box closed had turned it into Mary Poppins's carpet bag—it held any number of things.

I noticed that a corner of packing tape had peeled backward, collecting dust and fluff on its exposed sticky side, so it wouldn't stick down again when I pushed it. I went to the kitchen, pulled a roll of tape out of the drawer, and cut a length of it with my teeth. I stuck it over the loose corner, making sure it was shut.

★ ★ ★

You are in the supermarket doing some food shopping, and you have yogurt on your list. You go to the dairy section and notice that among the multiple brands and varieties, one type of yogurt is almost out of stock. You reach your arm right to the back of the shelf and find only two tubs left.

What conclusions can you draw from this? Maybe it's an especially delicious kind of yogurt that other people love, and you should try. Possibly you think that if you don't buy the last few tubs now, you won't have another chance. Or maybe this yogurt is a real bargain—the price is lower than it should be for such a good product.

When American researchers ran this as an experiment, they found that people's preferences for yogurt changed depending on how many were left.[1] When their favorite yogurt was abundant, they bought an ordinary amount of it. But when there weren't many left, their tastes seemed to change: They wanted more of the scarce yogurt than before.

We have all seen examples of this in real life. Think about the infamous toilet roll shortage at the beginning of the 2020 pandemic. There were people who wanted to buy more toilet paper after seeing pictures of the empty shelves in supermarkets, even though they already had enough for themselves at home. Suppliers said there was plenty to go around for everyone, but the madness of our purchasing behavior created a shortage.

Similarly, over the years people have camped out overnight for the chance to buy the latest iPhone on the day of its release, knowing that only a set number is available. After frenzies in previous years, customers know that they will have to do something drastic to get one of the few phones available—and conclude that there must be something very important about having a slightly better camera and a slightly sharper screen if other people are willing to wait all night to get one.

Scarcity seems to fog up our minds when it comes to shopping for and owning stuff. We don't wonder whether that type of yogurt is scarce because it goes sour too quickly and the supermarket has had to throw lots of it away; we don't consider whether queuing to buy something simply means that the company is not very good at managing its supply chains. Instead, we see scarcity as a good thing: When something is rare, we want it more, but when it's abundant, we're not as bothered. Why is that? In the five decades since scarcity theory was first formulated, there has been a huge amount of research into these questions.

What Does Scarcity Do to Our Minds?

Everyone has felt scarcity—defined as having less of something than we need—throughout their lives, although it clearly affects some people more acutely. It has a "tunneling" effect on our focus, stripping back our ability to think about anything other than the one thing that we're short of. If there is plenty of food in the cupboards but a power outage means that you can't turn on the lights, you don't spend time thinking about how you have plenty of cereal bars to eat. All your attention will be turned toward the thing you need but don't have: electricity.

Two of the key researchers on the topic of scarcity are Eldar Shafir and Sendhil Mullainathan, two professors who have written dozens of papers and a book that seek to describe how our behavior changes when we are faced with limited resources.

In one experiment they did with coauthor Anuj Shah, they asked participants to play a video game, like *Angry Birds*, where you fire shots at targets.[2] They divided the group in two: the "rich" were given 150 shots to complete the round, and the "poor" had just 30 shots. They found that the shot-poor group spent much more time aiming to get the perfect shot, using their shots as a precious resource that they wanted to use carefully. The rich group, on the other hand, fired willy-nilly and were far less accurate.

Four Theories for Why You Might Be Struggling with Scarcity

Shopping "festivals" like Prime Day or Black Friday encourage people to buy more by using the principles of scarcity, offering discounts that are limited by time. This tactic can be staggeringly effective. In 2021, Chinese consumers spent $84.5 billion on the megaretailer Alibaba during the shopping festival Singles Day (November 11).[3] To put that number into context, $84.5 billion was almost as much as the GDP of the entire country of Sri Lanka that year.[4]

Dr. Caroline Roux, a marketing professor at Concordia University in Montreal, Canada, has dedicated her career to studying how resource scarcity affects people's behavior. She says that making products feel scarce by giving customers limited opportunities to buy things can be an effective way to encourage them to buy more. Think of those Black Friday sales: The products themselves are not scarce (you can buy them all year round), but your opportunity to buy them for a lower price is.

Say there's a great TV that's on a Black Friday sale for half its recommended retail price. For everyone who can't afford one at its full price, the set available in this limited window of opportunity suddenly becomes very valuable indeed, representing the only opportunity you might have to own a good TV. "So that's when the value I think goes up suddenly for the same product,"

Dr. Roux says. "[Before] it was seen as valuable, but not as something I had to fight for because I couldn't afford it."

COMMODITY THEORY

Commodity theory was one of the first ways of thinking about scarcity and stuff after the publication of the 1968 essay "Implications of Commodity Theory for Value Change" by Timothy C. Brock, a social psychologist at Ohio State University.[5] It puts forward that we value commodities (any product or thing for which we have a use) by how scarce they are, with the rarest items being seen as the most valuable. This, of course, chimes with what we just learned in the chapter about social status—that status symbols tend to be things that are hard to get hold of.

Brock also notes that our attitudes toward stuff are mediated by the level of threat we are currently feeling. When we "anticipate decrement in physical or social well-being," we hold on to our stuff more tightly and are less willing to share with others. Brock's original work doesn't test reasons why this might be the case, although he does speculate that we might be driven to like scarce items because of our built-in desire to feel unique.

In 1970 this theory was tested.[6] The researcher told participants that they were enrolled in a study about inducing psychedelic-like experiences. In a classic psychology research trick, the experiment in fact started much earlier, when the subjects were asked to fill in a questionnaire about their personality traits, interests, and values. They were then given bogus results from these forms, being told that either they scored a little similarly to others or very similarly. After that, they were given a choice of four "audio-visual-olfactory-tactile-kinetic experiences" that were meant to mimic the effects of psychedelic drugs.

The researchers found that the people who were told they were very similar to others reacted badly. In a quest to regain their sense of individuality, they were far more likely to choose the experience that had very limited availability times over the experience that was open all week. After being told they were like everyone else, they were keen to find another way to demonstrate their uniqueness, and they saw the scarce thing as a way of doing it.

I feel the pull of unique and scarce items when shopping in thrift stores. There is something almost magical about rifling through the racks and finding a dress that fits you perfectly, a feeling that fate has smiled on you and put that dress there just for you to find. I am guilty of feeling a little smug when someone asks me where an item comes from and I say "a thrift store," knowing that they will not be able to copy me and buy the same.

An example of this gone wrong is the Zara dress that went viral in the United Kingdom in 2019. It was white with small black spots, loose, ran to the midcalf, and had three-quarter length sleeves. Zara won't say how many they sold, but as someone who was in London over that summer, I can say it was a lot; so many, in fact, that an Instagram account called @hot4thespot was set up for pictures of people wearing it. Women arrived for lunch with a friend to realize they were both wearing it; I saw pictures of a dozen women wearing it at a festival; the press called it the "$50 dress that conquered Britain."[7] There were three women in my office who had it, and one day they all wore it on the same day.

But after the initial rush, the ubiquity became a turnoff. After that hilarious day when all three of my colleagues wore it, I hardly saw "The Dress" in the office again. While we may want to follow fashion in our own subtle way, no one wants to feel like they're just directly copying everyone else.

CONFORMITY THEORY

The other side of the coin is conformity theory. Although we want to feel that we're unique and special individuals, we don't want that feeling to be so extreme that we don't fit in or feel cast out of a social group. The desire for both uniqueness and belonging is a fine balance, and having the same things as others can help us to feel that we fit in, as well as signaling which tribe we're in.

The great journalist Joan Didion built a career writing about the huge social upheavals of the 1960s and 1970s and the cultural divides they brought, covering everything from California hippies to Republican National Conventions. In *The White Album* she wrote about the packing list she used when preparing a bag for overnight reporting trips, which included clothes, notebooks, and toiletries, as well as cigarettes and whiskey. The contents of the bag were chosen to help her to blend into different social groups: "In a skirt, a leotard, and stockings, I could pass on either side of the culture," she wrote.[8] Either consciously or subconsciously, we all use similar principles to blend in with others, or to show that we're part of a certain culture or subculture. Conformity theory explains that our desire to be like others, or to be accepted by others, can make scarce things more appealing as we assume that something is rare because it's popular with other people.

Think about a restaurant with people queuing outside for a table. Tables are scarce, and we therefore assume that the restaurant must be really good—even if it could just be a sign that their booking system has crashed. Venues frequently use this principle to their advantage by falsely creating queues to create buzz around them, like the nightclub in southwest London I went to with three friends a few years ago. Our excitement built as we lined up, listening to the thrumming music coming from inside. But when the bouncer finally let us in, we found the place almost completely empty, with just half a dozen people in there! We spent the rest of the night in stitches of laughter at the empty dance floor, then hid in the corner from embarrassment. We had been so easily conned.

AVOIDING REGRET

I have plenty of regrets about the stuff I own: I can regret not snapping up a bargain in the sale just as much as I rue all the mindless shopping for fast fashion that I did in my early twenties.

Research shows that regret is one of the most powerful psychological drivers, and it can stick in our minds for decades. We usually can't resolve our regrets by giving them a different ending—what's done is done, and we just have to accept it.

Given how painful and irritating regrets can be, people often go far out of their way to avoid them. This, unfortunately, doesn't help us make sensible decisions around scarce items when shopping. Knowing that the supply of something is limited can make us want it even more, thinking that we will regret not doing so later, when the opportunity has passed.

Professor Feng Li of Bayes Business School researches the use of scarcity in marketing. He also has personal experience of this effect, having grown up under communism in China, where, he says, "things [were] cheap, but you just [didn't] have enough of them." Basic supplies like food were severely limited, with rationing in place to spread out the meager reserves.

Li remembers queuing with his family outside shops for their chance to buy whatever was in stock before it ran out. If, say, the shop that day had just cooking oil and salt, his family would buy them—even if they already had enough at home. "Whenever you [saw] something . . . You go there and get it because after that you might not be able to get it [later]," he says. The unpredictability of supplies actually made the shortages worse: People would rush out and buy whatever there was, whether or not they needed it. Buying oil and salt whenever they saw it helped them to maintain some control over their environment and reduced their likelihood of being met with scarcity later on.

REACTANCE THEORY

Another way of understanding how scarcity affects our decisions around stuff is reactance theory, which is the idea that people have a natural inclination toward freedom and act negatively when they feel that choices are being taken away. It's the theory that explains why we rail against disciplinarian teachers; why we fall for reverse psychology; why being told to tidy our rooms makes us tetchy.

In scarcity research, reactance comes into play when the lack of an object restricts our ability to choose. A good example is how we tend to act like naughty children when our access to films, TV, or music is limited: We want the forbidden fruit simply because it's forbidden. In the United States, NBC had the exclusive right to broadcast the 2008 Beijing Olympics. Given the twelve-hour time difference between the East Coast and Beijing, getting decent audience numbers was challenging, so they decided to delay broadcast of the opening ceremony until later in the day when more Americans would be at home and ready to watch.

But Americans did not like being told to wait. They searched the internet for streaming websites hosted in Europe, while NBC frantically asked the websites to shut down access to American viewers. It was described as a four-hour "digital whack-a-mole," which ultimately backfired on NBC.[9] "In the end, it appears that NBC's act of censorship actually increased interest in live viewing for many Web users, consistent with reactance theory," concluded a 2009 paper.[10]

A 1977 study looked at an example of this that we find in our day-to-day lives: how children act when they are told that they can't have a certain toy.[11] Like many of you, I spent my childhood running this experiment, in my case with my sister, and although we didn't get our results peer reviewed, we discovered that a sibling holding a toy makes you want to play with it a hell of a lot more.

How Scarcity Theories Are Used
by Business

The luxury goods market is full of successful applications of the principles of scarcity in shopping, like the Birkin bags that we looked at earlier. But it's not necessarily just at the top of the market where retailers create scarcity.

I used to be a sucker for shopping in places that sold branded clothes at heavily discounted prices. The problem with these stores (at least for me) is that they make it very tricky to make good decisions. For example, a few years ago I went shopping in one of these places and found a single pair of pink camouflage-print leggings from a well-known brand that were 50 percent off. It was clear why they hadn't been sold at full price—as I say, they were pink camouflage print—but there was something alluring about them anyway. They were the only pair left in any size, and if I didn't buy them right then, someone else would come along and snap them up. I bought them, took them home, and put them in a drawer, where they stayed for some years.

Jake McKenzie's business, Intermark Group, is built around helping companies use scarcity and nearly one hundred other psychological principles in how they market to consumers. As he begins to describe his work to me, it's like he's telling me an incredibly obvious truth: Scarcity marketing is everywhere.

The other day, I was buying concert tickets for myself and three friends. As I was dithering about which seats to buy, the screen showed me a timer counting down—either I put down the money in the next ten minutes, or I would lose the seats to someone else. That's scarcity marketing, says McKenzie: Even if the venue had only sold half their tickets, that timer will make you think that your opportunity to buy tickets is brief and limited.

McKenzie says that another way in which companies quietly appeal to your sense of scarcity is when they tell you how many units of something are left. Do you have any idea of typical stock levels for a particular T-shirt in a particular color in a particular size? Probably not. So there's no reason that it should scare you when there are "fewer than 100 remaining." Maybe they only ordered one hundred in the first place.

Also, the phrase "last remaining" might not mean what you think it does. Perhaps in the shop's stockroom there are fewer than one hundred of those T-shirts, but maybe there's a shipment arriving in an hour, or there are a thousand more in a warehouse that they hire rather than own, so they can technically say that the items are not in stock with them. "It is just a completely meaningless phrase," says McKenzie.

The Value of Plentiful Things

All this brings me back to that box of hair ties from the top of the chapter. When you get hundreds of hair ties in a box, you don't stop to consider the value of just one, like I rarely consider the huge benefit of being able to turn on my tap and get as many glasses of fresh water as I like. When something is abundant it becomes static in the background. We take it for granted so much that we stop noticing that it's even there.

This connects with the experiment we looked at earlier, about the people who were assigned to play the *Angry Birds*–style game with either plenty of shots or few of them. Although the group with scarce shots got too focused on their short-term performance in each round, not thinking about the game overall, the group with many shots didn't fare particularly well either: Their shots were plentiful, and so they took little care when using them.

But this meant that they weren't very accurate, and although the rich group had five times as many shots as the poor group, their sloppy approach ensured they did not get five times as many points. The authors say that "if the 'rich' had played as if they were 'poor,' they would have performed better."

"It seems that to understand the psychology of scarcity, we must also appreciate the psychology of abundance," they add. 'If scarcity can engage us too much, abundance might engage us too little."[12]

In other words, it's not just scarcity that makes us act weirdly around our possessions; abundance can too. Scarce things aren't necessarily the most important things we have, and abundant things aren't worthless. But our brains have evolved this shortcut so that we pay attention to shortages that could become dangerous. It is still a markedly useful way of acting when things we need are scarce—if the taps run dry, we will focus very hard on finding a source of water—but not so much around things that we don't need.

★ ★ ★

We want to be unique individuals, and the same as our peers; we want to stand out, yet fit in; we want to own distinctive things, and also what everyone else has. Scarce things can sway our minds by appealing to all of these competing desires, promising to give us all the impossible things that we want.

But something being rare or plentiful does not reflect its value. Just because that dress was the last one left on sale doesn't mean you should buy it. Does it fit? Do you like how you feel in it? And just because you bought those pretty patterned wine glasses in a supermarket doesn't mean you should treat them like they're worthless. If you love them, that's great! Take care of them.

Objects should add value to our lives, making them easier or more fun. Rarity is irrelevant.

FINAL THOUGHTS

BE CAREFUL WITH DISCOUNT SHOPPING

Unless we set our minds to it, it is very difficult to separate out our judgment of an item from the circumstances in which we found it. This can be particularly difficult when shopping in discount stores or at sales, where a feeling of scarcity can make us impulsive. As much as you can, try to go into discount shopping with a plan of what you want or need to buy, and try to stick to it as far as possible.

Ask yourself whether you would still be tempted to buy an item at its full price. If not, then it probably isn't a good idea to buy it at a discount either—you are probably reacting to the feeling of scarcity rather than the actual item in front of you.

BE AWARE OF FALSE SCARCITY

Browse on a couple of websites for something to buy—say, a lawnmower. Look around until you find a lawnmower that says it is "low stock," "going fast," or "last few," then save the URL somewhere. Come back a few days later and check the link. Is that lawnmower still available? Try a couple of other examples too. It's remarkable how often something being marked as "going fast" seems to have no impact on how difficult it actually is to buy.

EXPERIMENT WITH LIMITING YOUR SUPPLIES

If an item is relatively cheap, and you often have a lot of it on hand, experiment by restricting how much of it is available to you at any one time. After the hair tie incident, I bought myself a strip of ten and told myself I would have to look after them, as I wouldn't buy any more for the year. Of the ten, I put half in my bedside table, allowing myself to have only five out at once. It was remarkably effective—I developed a sixth sense for knowing where every single one of them was at any time. One could be on my desk at work, another in my gym bag, one on my wrist, and two in my chest of drawers. Five was more than enough.

You Are Not What You Own

The most vivid memories I have of being a teenager are of shopping. My friends Millie, Issy, and I would arrive at 4 p.m. still in our school uniform and wander around Topshop, pointing out the things we liked to each other. Those afternoons were like a series of field research trips: We were there to find out about adulthood. We looked in each shop, assessing the options. Did we want to be slick, chic career women in cigarette pants, or creative souls with long necklaces and billowing sleeves?

One Christmas we went shopping in London, spending a few hours trailing in and out of vintage shops, discovering even more options. I have a precious photo of Millie and me from that day taken in a fitting room. I'm wearing a hideous blue 1980s top, sequins eddying all over it, shoulder pads wide enough to bridge the Atlantic. Millie is wearing a sparkly silver sack that dwarfs her slight frame, and at her hips turns abruptly into a black cow-spot pattern. We strike spiky, rigid poses and draw our lips forward into tight pouts, daring the camera to catch us at our worst.

We understood the fun of dressing up; how we could use clothes as an experiment, testing ourselves, finding our true desires.

★ ★ ★

I got the tiny handbag for my birthday the summer before I went to university. It was roughly square in shape, covered in silver beads, and had a clasp at the top that snapped shut like jaws. It was so small that I couldn't close it when my phone was inside, which meant that it usually hung over my shoulder, its mouth hanging slackly open. It showed wear quickly, the beads dropping off with the slightest friction or hanging loosely from strings, revealing white satin beneath. One night, I dropped it after a few drinks. The force of the fall knocked open the lid of some eyeshadow that was inside. It broke into dust, coating the clean white lining with coruscant gold.

I adored it. I loved how it was so impractical, prioritizing sparkle over utility. It put fun first.

★ ★ ★

My sister likes to tease me about a lot of things, including the clothes I wear. I like what I think of as timeless styles—classical shapes, well-cut skirts, good quality fabrics. This is not how she sees things.

"You look like such a . . . millennial," she told me one day. Rosie is six years younger than me, which means she is on the other side of the generational watershed in Gen Z. On the day she tells me this, she is wearing what she thinks is a normal outfit: gym leggings, a band T-shirt, and a hoodie so big it reaches almost to her knees.

I looked down at my own clothes. I was wearing a brown circle skirt, white pussy-bow blouse, and black ballet pumps. I had no idea what she was talking about.

The Stages of a Trend

One of the best explanations of the mechanics of trends is in the 2006 film *The Devil Wears Prada*, starring Meryl Streep as Miranda Priestly, the fearsome editor of a glossy magazine, and Anne Hathaway, who plays Andy, her fashion-skeptic assistant. When putting together a look, Andy snorts as Priestly hesitates between two blue-green belts, which Andy claims "look exactly the same to me." Priestly refuses to accept Andy's dismissal and launches into a monologue that explains the inner workings of the fashion industry. As an example, Priestly explains how the exact cerulean shade of Andy's jumper came from a 2002 cat-walk look by Oscar de la Renta, which later trickled into Yves Saint Laurent. It then went through eight other designers before sparking trends in department stores, where it "trickled on down into some tragic casual corner where you, no doubt, fished it out of some clearance bin." Mocking people who work in fashion is ridiculous, concludes Priestly—given the power they have on the outfit that Andy herself is wearing.

This speech is the turn in the film, the inflection point where Andy begins to cast off her snobbery and internalized sexism and take the people she works with more seriously. She is right to do so—Priestly implicitly understands several psychological and sociological theories about how trends work.

Priestly was explaining the theory of the diffusion of innovations, first popularized in a 1962 book of the same name by Everett Rogers, who was at the time an academic at Ohio State University. Detailing a five-step process, he tried to explain how innovations—which could be as concrete as a new technology, or as abstract as an idea or trend—spread through society, turning from a niche concept to a rapidly spreading trend.

At the beginning are the innovators: the people who originate new trends. They are a specialized group, perhaps only a few percent of the population. They have very different mindsets to the rest of us—they are constantly open to new ideas and willing to take financial and social risks on things that might be a complete disaster. Think of the first people to bring back flares when everyone was wearing skinny jeans. They may have been thought lame or tragic by some, and yet they ignored the views of everyone around them, believing they saw something that no one else could.

The early adopters are a group who don't come up with new ideas but are very sensitive to emerging trends. Rather than originators, they are more like connoisseurs who select the best of the new things they see and communicate them to a wider group.

After that, a trend starts to peak as the majority cottons on. These are the people who don't like to take risks, and who prefer to wait until an idea is tried and tested before giving it a go, perhaps preferring to stay hidden as part of the crowd.

And then, at the end, are the remaining sliver of people known as laggards, who might refuse to follow a trend at all, or hold out until the last moment before adopting it. There is one person in my life who I think very much fits this description. He is in his late twenties, but his habits make him seem decades older. He always carries cash, writes with a fountain pen, ignores all trends, refuses to buy a microwave, and drinks loose-leaf tea. He could have been living this very same lifestyle, by and large, many decades ago. If he buys a microwave, it will probably be thirty, forty, or sixty years after everyone else has realized how bloody helpful they are.

As a trend moves through these various stages, its popularity gradually rises, peaks, and then drops off. Trends tend to have the strongest appeal when they are on the way up, before reaching a saturation point where an item is "overexposed" and people feel tired of it. It then sinks into a period of obsolescence, where it will sit for a period of time before it becomes so forgotten that one of the cool innovators thinks it's time to bring it back again. To me, it feels like trends in fashion are spending less time in obsolescence now than ever before. When I was a teenager, 1980s trends had a resurgence. After thirty years of obsolescence, we got obsessed with big boxy denim jackets and loud sportswear. But now, trends that have spent just ten years in obsolescence can be resurrected. Only recently, I had lunch in a café where a teenage girl at the next table was wearing low-rise jeans, UGG boots, and a Juicy Couture hoodie: the look that I was rocking just ten or fifteen years ago. Clothes that I wore without thinking twice are already being worn by teenagers ironically.

★ ★ ★

This defiant attitude to dressing (and to life) has been taken on almost as a trend in itself, with a subculture of people using clothes to show that they do not get dressed to look nice for other people.

One brand currently at the forefront of this is OGBFF. It was started by two friends in Los Angeles who decided to print the funniest things they could think of onto clothes. For around fifty dollars, you can be the owner of a T-shirt that says "No one actually likes Aperol Spritz" or "Niche Internet micro celebrity." For seventy dollars, you can own a miniskirt printed with the words "Mini skirt." According to a profile, the idea came one evening when the two of them were eating Taco Bell and mucking about on Photoshop creating silly slogans.[1] At first they printed the T-shirts just for themselves, before selling them informally to friends and on Depop. From the beginning it was an insular project, one long inside joke designed to be confusing to outsiders.

The idea that neither the designer nor wearer is trying to win your approval is part of the appeal. The pair told the magazine that someone wearing OGBFF is the type who is "the funniest person in the room but in no rush to prove it."

I have another theory of ironic clothing. I think that wearing clothes that make you look bad could actually be a way of showing off. If you've gone out in a dad fleece and Crocs, and you still look hot, then you must be *really* hot. You don't even have to try. It feels similar to that phase when tech bros went around wearing slouchy jeans, scruffy T-shirts, and hoodies: Their heedlessness about how they came across was a way to show how important they were at work. They didn't even have to dress properly and yet could still earn huge salaries.

Speaking with Clothes

On paper, Sian Clarke is a stylist, but after hearing her talk about her job, I could give her a few other labels too: psychologist, emotional support worker, professional friend. Clients come to her saying they need advice about their wardrobes, but underneath there are usually a host of other concerns too. "Usually they reach out because of change, like a job promotion, getting married, finishing having children; but sometimes it's traumatic events like divorce, loss, or breakdowns," she says. Their lives have changed, and they have had to rapidly become another person. They want to communicate those changes to the world.

Clarke tends to work with people in a standardized way, beginning with a "wardrobe edit": going through items they own one by one and identifying the things they want to hold on to, and the things they don't. This in itself is usually an emotional experience, with each item sparking feelings of pride or shame, memories of joy or despair. The stories come thick and fast, with tales of much-loved dresses that were worn on first dates with their now-husbands, or shirts to avoid forever after they were worn at a funeral. It can be a superstitious, even slightly mystical, process, says Clarke: "Sometimes people won't wear a dress because the last time they wore it something bad happened." This can be even more potent with clothes that were bought vintage: "These clothes have had an amazing life before you, and you don't even know what stories they hold," she says.

The next step is to think about what the client is trying to achieve. Sometimes it can be very practical, like putting together an outfit for a big event. But sometimes her clients want to achieve a particular emotional state and are using clothes as a way of getting there. Life changes have shaken up their old ways of living, and they turn to clothes to help them feel settled, comforted, or in control. New jobs are a common theme, says Clarke: "It's a whole thing with imposter syndrome: They feel that 'If I dress for this job that I've somehow wangled, people won't find out that I don't belong here.'" She might first reassure them that their fears of not deserving the job are unfounded, but that wearing a "big outfit for a big job" might help to assuage their worries.

A divorce, which can be even more unsettling, will often prompt someone to consult Clarke as they seek comfort and succor. "Normally their confidence is at rock bottom; they've gone through this trauma that they never thought would happen, and they're trying to build their confidence back up," she says. It's never "a full transformation; it's a slower process, more of a healing process to build them back up, and giving them the tools [for] when they feel ready to go back out there dating or literally just out with friends. They've changed so they will want to look different . . . [They think] 'I feel awful but I'm ready to feel good again.' It's finding the 2.0 version of you."

A few years ago, Clarke had a client who came to her with an SOS call—she was going to a wedding and knew her ex would be there. "She said, 'I want to look very hot, but like I've made absolutely no effort whatsoever.'" Clarke helped her select a dress and accessories that made her stand out, but not too much, in colors that were cheery and bright while suiting her complexion. It worked a treat: She could relax knowing that she looked and felt good about herself. "She said she'd never looked better or had so many compliments," says Clarke.

I was, of course, interested in the clothes that Clarke herself was wearing and what she was trying to say with them. When we speak, she is wearing an example of what she calls her "creative" look, where she likes to play with mixing colors and patterns. On this day, it is a bright-blue shirt underneath an animal-print cardigan with a huge fluffy collar. She has big, wire-framed glasses that cover the middle third of her face. The top third is covered by a sandy fringe, with the rest of her hair tied back with a blue scarf.

This exuberant mix of things is what she wears day-to-day for work, almost like an advertisement for the joy and fun that can be had with dressing. She has other styles for other occasions too. For big events there is a "dramatic" style that is "glamorous and striking, more powerful, more head turning; when you're public speaking you need to be remembered." And then at weekends she has a "vintage, edgy style" that's more "pared down." She wants to send different messages at different times, and she understands that she can use clothes to do this.

So should you be dressing for yourself or for others? Is the confidence boost internal, or does it also affect how we come across to others? Of course, knowing that you look good, like the woman at the wedding, will make you feel confident from the inside, says Clarke. "There's nothing better than putting something on and saying 'I love this,' and that radiates out from you." But we're all human. "Even if you're dressing for yourself, there's always a tiny part of you that wants other people to know."

★ ★ ★

Another way of thinking about this is to consider that our clothing and personal objects can—rightly or wrongly—send messages to others. In some cases, the messages can be very obvious. My mind turns to a T-shirt that my dad was once given at an event he worked at, which had "HERE TO HELP" printed on the back. For some unknown reason, he decided to wear it again on a day trip to London, where he was stopped all day long by people asking for directions. He was sending a message to others, but not the right one.

We can also use our things to send more helpful messages. A claddagh is an Irish traditional ring with a design showing two hands holding a heart that is topped with a crown. It is steeped in symbolism: The heart represents love, the hands friendship, and the crown loyalty. How it is worn is important too. It can be worn on the left hand, usually the ring finger, where the heart pointing outward toward the fingertips indicates engagement and pointing inward means that you are married. If worn on the right hand, however, it has different meanings—the heart pointing outward means that you are looking for love, and pointing inward means that you're in a relationship.[2]

Unexpected and Unfortunate Meanings of Clothes

Our clothes can also send messages that are so subtle they are received subconsciously, often without the wearer's knowledge. This is not always a good thing, as people can read baseless, inaccurate, or unfair meanings into the clothes we wear.

For example, our culture has woven a thick web of associations about the meanings and uses of different colors, and this can affect how people see us when we wear them. For example, red and black can make us look more attractive to potential partners.[3] Wearing those colors can have other effects too: Sports teams in black stripes are penalized more often than those in other colors, as they appear more malignant,[4] while red uniforms appear to give a competitive advantage in combat sports.[5] In a study about librarians, researchers from the University of Maine tested both formal and casual outfits in blue, white, and red to see how they affected people's judgment of character. They found that the blue options made the librarian seem most approachable, followed by the white options, and then the red, with the authors suggesting that red may have scored lowest because of its association "with the trait of dominance."[6]

Beyond color, how "formal" we rate someone's clothes to be can make a big difference to the impressions we form of them. An influential study from 1971 found that someone's clothing even affects how we treat them.[7] Researchers dressed in different outfits stationed themselves in Grand Central Station and JFK Airport in New York. They left dimes in the change slots of phone booths and walked away, then waited for the next person to come and use the booth. After a few minutes, they would return and ask the person whether they had seen a dime that they had left behind.

When the researchers wore "high-status" clothes—suits and ties for men and neat dresses and smart coats for women—the dimes were returned 77 percent of the time. But when the same people wore "low-status" clothes—the men dressed as workers, the women looking "generally unkempt in appearance," people gave the money back only 38 percent of the time. "When the subjects thought they were dealing with a high status person, they returned the dime more than twice as often as when they perceived the stimulus person to be of low status," concluded the study. The enormous difference between these two rates feels both surprising and saddening—why take the money of someone who looks like they need it the most?

A range of studies has shown how the formality of clothing can also make someone appear to have certain personality traits. One study found that a stranger wearing conservative but casual clothes was judged to be more reliable, self-controlled, and understanding; someone in "daring" clothes was seen as individualistic and attractive; and someone in "dressy" clothes was considered to be dependent on others and not at ease socially.[8]

It's possible to imagine a scenario that somehow links these traits to clothes—perhaps only someone who doesn't care about what others think could wear daring outfits—but a lot of the time these inferences are wrong. Sometimes it's just laundry day. At its worst, misreading someone's outfit choice can cause serious harm, as with the flawed reasoning that a woman's sexual desires can be understood from what she wears.

A Self That Lives On

Our feeling that you can know a person by looking at their things extends to our obsession with visiting the homes of famous dead people. Each year, more than half a million people visit Graceland, Elvis Presley's home in Memphis, Tennessee, where they feel they come closer to understanding the singer by seeing the stained glass, mirrored ceilings, bright colors, and busy wallpapers.[9] Personally, I felt a richer understanding of Beatrix Potter after going to Hill Top, the farm where she lived in the Lake District in the north of England. Potter lived until 1943, but the downstairs of her house looks like it was last touched hundreds of years ago, given its dark seventeenth- and eighteenth-century Lakeland furniture. Upstairs there is something quite different: the whimsical "treasure room," where dozens of tiny animal figurines are displayed in glass cases. The house seemed to say two things about her: She loved nature and traditional ways of living.

That form of self-expression, via our homes, could be seen as a search for permanence in a shifting world. Graceland and Hill Top carry the character of their famous inhabitants—the flamboyance of Elvis, Beatrix Potter's quiet passions. The things they collected in their homes feel like a way of proving who they were to the external world, of showing others that they had lived. I was struck by a piece in the *Financial Times* about the places where bestselling female authors write, and how they have chosen to decorate their little corners of the world. Some of them write from the kitchen table, while others use specific desks in studies full of books, trinkets, and postcards that inspire them. These decorated surroundings give Mieko Kawakami, author of *Breasts and Eggs*, a sense of permanence in an otherwise finite life. "I'll be gone someday, and all that will be left of me will be my things," she says. "No matter how long your soul wants to live, you can only go on as long as your body lets you—it's a limited resource."[10]

It feels like if we express who we are with objects then we can extend our longevity a little, with part of us living on after we've gone. When I've died, I won't be able to crack a joke with friends, but I hope that some of my sense of humor might be expressed through the embroidered cat in a bright-blue frame in my living room. I hope that my collection of books will reveal what I was interested in, and my box of photos convey what I thought were the most important moments of my life.

Perhaps this makes sense. We regularly use the objects that last to build pictures of what historical figures were like, sometimes sketching portraits from very little. One of the victims of the AD 79 volcanic eruption of Mount Vesuvius was a woman aged approximately forty-five whose body was found in Herculaneum. While all that was left of her was a skeleton, some of her stuff remained in near-pristine condition. Slipped onto the blackened bones of her fingers were two shining gold rings studded with red and green gemstones. Next to her body were two gold bracelets and a bag of coins. From these few facts alone people have tried to construct a story about the woman, who is sometimes imagined to have been a rich individual who didn't flee with the other wealthy inhabitants of the town. Her belongings have become synonymous with who she is: She is referred to as the "ring lady of Herculaneum." So even if our belongings do survive us, we can see that without us around to explain them, the stories they tell about who we were won't necessarily be accurate. They will be like stars in the sky, which others join together to make constellations.

In fact, it is rare for objects to be preserved as well as the Herculaneum jewelry. And while it is true that our bodies won't last forever, objects won't either. Even with museum-quality preservation, they will fade and decline and fall apart eventually. And our things will almost certainly not be preserved that well. A few will be kept by our loved ones, while the rest will be given away or sold. If I'm lucky, the embroidered cat will go to a thrift store where its silliness and fun will endure, but as a message without a source. But more likely it will go in the garbage.

★ ★ ★

The feeling of incongruity or surprise as our look completely changes—whether borrowing clothes from a friend or trying on a new outfit in a shop—can sometimes be very welcome, if we are trying to find a new style, but other times it can just feel discombobulating. Sometimes you don't want to be conscious of the clothes you have on—you want them to fade into the background, below the level of your noticing. You want them to feel as natural as any other part of you.

I have an oversized pink shirt with black dots. It is shiny, jolly, and a bit silly. When I'm wearing it, I can look in the mirror and see myself looking back. I am instantly comfortable: the soft, easy feeling of coming home after a long day. I have similar feelings toward some things in my flat. On Gumtree I found an old pine desk with twisted legs that someone had painted yellow in a slightly slapdash way, with one side coming out a little brighter than the other. It feels completely right in my home, as if I have had it forever, like I painted it myself. The shirt and the desk are not for everyone, but they are certainly for me. Parting with either would feel like losing a family member. We clearly belong together.

Making things work primarily for ourselves seems like the best way of doing things—although of course we have all been caught up in trends at some point. As we have seen, it's natural to pay attention to what others are doing and to let that affect our behavior, to an extent. I also don't think it's always a bad thing—standing completely apart from the world sounds like a lot of effort. But I do think it is good to stop being dragged back and forth by trends, of buying or wearing things that we don't truly love. There is space to interpret every trend in our own way.

FINAL THOUGHTS

THINKING IN DIFFERENT TIME SCALES

There are ways that we can distance ourselves from the pressure of trends, like using the perspective of time. When you are out shopping and drawn to an item, try to imagine how you would have seen the same thing a year ago, or five or ten years ago. If it would have been with utter horror, bemusement, or revulsion, please put it down. You will feel utter horror, bemusement, or revulsion toward it again soon.

WHAT OBJECTS MAKE YOU FEEL LIKE YOURSELF?

I would love for you to take stock of the things you own and wear and think about which of them give you that deep sense of belonging and self-recognition. If someone who knew you well were to go through your wardrobe and put together an outfit that is you in a nutshell, what would they pick? Similarly, if they were to make a TV show about you, what items would they include in the set for it to feel authentically like your place?

On the other hand, what do you own that makes you feel the opposite—something that makes its presence known in a slightly annoying way, and makes you feel slightly stiff? Are you sure you want such things in your life?

CHARACTER CREATION

One morning, pause for a moment after you've gotten dressed, and consider what you've put on. Try to explain out loud why you have chosen each item, going into as much detail as possible about what you're trying to do with each element. These normally unspoken explanations can be illuminating. Here is me, by way of example:

- Blue jersey dress: I feel like it's a good balance between being flattering and looking like I haven't tried too hard to look nice. Plus, much faster to put on in the morning than thinking about putting together an outfit from tops and bottoms.
- Black leather loafers: bought because my old shoes were wearing out and I worried they made me look like I didn't care enough about my job.
- Gold hoop earrings: softly accentuate my outfit without being too eye-catching.
- Thermal vest: It's cold.

My motivations for the day quickly become clear: I want to be respected at work, and look good, while doing so subtly and with ease. Just like on those teenage shopping trips, I have figured out who I want to be.

RULES OF DRESSING

Think about the rules you have absorbed around the clothes you wear and how you look. Perhaps this is best achieved by going into a shop: Pick up something that you would never usually buy, and try to explain why that is. You will probably come up with some bizarre rules that sound like they're cast-iron despite just being based on offhand comments you heard decades ago. By doing this exercise, I realized that I never wear red (in my head, the combination of red with my blonde hair makes me look like stripes of ketchup and mustard on a hot dog); I avoid trousers (must hide size of thighs); and I'm cautious of jumpsuits (uncomfortable when you have a very long torso). The last of these makes some sense, but the others are barriers that I've created to help me avoid feeling unattractive and to protect myself from humiliation.

Although the realization that I had set myself rules unconsciously didn't immediately change the contents of my wardrobe, it has at least helped me to be a little more open-minded. If I see a red sweater that I love, I will try it on and see how it looks before immediately discounting it. There is also a subtle benefit, as it frees your perception of yourself. You don't need to restrict yourself or hide in a corner.

WHAT WILL YOU LEAVE BEHIND?

Look around at your things, and consider what messages you are trying to convey with them. Are there important parts of yourself that you haven't managed to express to others with words? I find it difficult or embarrassing to explain the floatier parts of my personality that allow me to read happily for hours or let my feet and mind wander as I enjoy a long walk alone. For a long time I tried to do this with the lighthearted way I decorated my flat, hoping that the fact that my TV sits on a stack of books instead of a stand would get it across. If I couldn't say those things, then hopefully I could show them.

Perhaps you are also using your home to show visitors things about yourself: a passion for photography, from the images displayed on the walls; or for cooking, via your collection of cookbooks in the kitchen.

How would it feel to leave behind this cache of things after you pass away? And how would you feel if you *couldn't* leave it behind; if, say, you too lost your things in a fire? Are there parts of your personality that you would feel weren't being fully expressed without your things?

Collecting Is More Than Buying Stuff

I have never had the money nor the perseverance to be a proper collector. When I was a child, I had a Harry Potter sticker book that I started in earnest but never completed after realizing it would take six months of pocket money to do so. As an adult, I kept a purse tucked away in a drawer that contained a few dozen fifty-pence coins with special designs on them. I wasn't bothered about their value, or even the history or sport of coin collecting. They just felt too special to spend like normal money, so I kept them.

Other half-baked collections included a small box of post-cards that I brought back from my travels. Every time I went away I would buy a few, bring them home, and then put them in the box. It was like having a photo album, but lazy. It was totally worthless and wasn't even pretty or impressive to look at, but still there was a part of me that felt a twinge when I thought about getting rid of it.

Time went on. Six months after the fire I had pulled myself together enough to move out of my parents' house and into a flat in London, which I shared with one of my best friends.

My parents drove my two suitcases of clothes to London, a journey that reminded us of the day we moved everything to the storage unit, when the car was so stuffed full that you couldn't see out the back window. This time was different, with the box marked "RANDOM" on my lap, and my two suitcases rolling about the near-empty trunk, banging into each other when the car turned sharply. All the way, the three of us took turns making variations of the same joke: Isn't moving so much easier when you don't own anything?

When we arrived, I waved them off, then wheeled my suitcases into my bedroom and left them there—I no longer had a wardrobe, so I couldn't put anything away. I sat on the hard wooden floor of my new room and made a list of things I needed to buy.

Through a small insurance policy, I'd been paid a sum that covered less than a third of the value of what I had lost, and I used this to replace the most pressing stuff. A friend of a friend offered me a bed, and also a sofa, which I put in the living room with a table and mismatched chairs I found in a junk shop. I picked up a mirror someone had left on the street and hung it in the bathroom. I bought one set of cutlery, some plates and bowls, and curtains for my bedroom. Then I was out of money. Everything else had to wait, leaving me with bare walls, hard rugless floors, and shadeless light bulbs.

Even after a few weeks the rooms still felt baggy and unfamiliar. I lived out of suitcases butterflied open on the floor, and the rooms echoed without any stuff around to soften the noise. I kept catching my sleeve on the same door handle and mixing up the cupboards for plates and mugs, as if my mind hadn't yet caught up with the fact that this was now my home. I wondered if the feeling might have something to do with the hard and unwelcoming surfaces, free of anything that marked me out as me.

One day I popped into a thrift store on a whim while waiting for a bus and rifled through a box of discarded knickknacks. I picked up a tiny vase with gold detailing, then a china figurine of a black cat. Everything in the box was one pound: If I wanted to, I could buy it all and refill my shelves in an instant. I carefully turned the trinkets and bibelots over in my hands. I left without buying a thing.

Despite feeling so listless and lost since the fire, there had been a few times over the months when I had had a glimmer of something else: I had a rare chance to start from scratch. I would never again hold on to a second can opener in case the first one broke. I had no photo frames that needed dusting or fancy wine glasses that needed hand-washing. I could pause and think and work out what more, if anything, I needed.

There were two ways to read that feeling of not yet being home. I could tell myself my home was gone forever, and feel disorientated and unsettled. Or I could see it as the good kind of time away from home—a vacation. It could be a break from my normal life. And, though I felt guilty admitting it, there had been times through the heartbreak when I had felt lighter without *some* of my things. Possessions can fix a memory, for good or bad. They make one version of the past permanent, giving it an outsize importance that it hasn't earned, while other memories fall away.

Take the box of postcards. It helped me remember some of the places I'd been on special trips, but it told me nothing about what my day-to-day life was like in the past. And with every postcard that I put into the shoebox I created a need to add more: I had accidentally created a tradition that now demanded my time and attention to shepherd it safely into the future. But for the time being, I didn't want any of that. I was too tender to give anything my care and attention.

For a while I was ruthless about making sure I wasn't building up another collection without noticing. Every Sunday, I tipped my handbag upside down and threw away every receipt and old ticket before they took on the gravitas of being from the past. When I went on vacation, I only bought postcards if I was going to write on and send them to friends. I didn't want another accidental collection, and deliberately starting one felt a bit pathetic: The first postcards would rattle around in the empty shoebox, all that empty space a baseless hope of something to come.

In the end, none of my deliberating mattered. My granny had heard about my empty flat and was determined to help. She had recently downsized, selling her family home and moving in with my aunty and uncle. With it, Granny had identified twin problems: She had a surplus of knickknacks, whereas I had a severe deficit of them. And so she dispatched a box of "emergency trinkets" to soften the hard edges of the flat. I was now the owner of a flowery vase, two mugs that commemorated the visit of Prince Charles to Wales in 1969, and a piece of china shaped like a horse and cart that may or may not be meant to hold a tea light. She threw in half a dozen small plates, just in case. Becoming the sudden owner of this little collection didn't feel odd at all.

★ ★ ★

One summer's day, I visited an auction house. The world of art and antiques is small and chatty, so I can't say which house it was, or the name of the auctioneer who showed me around. Let's call him Mark.

Mark has spent decades working with collectors of all kinds. Some collect antique furniture; others collect painfully niche types of china. Some have paintings, while others amass huge amounts of Victorian technical equipment. Whatever category of thing they have chosen to collect, they will go to extreme lengths to acquire it.

Part of Mark's job is valuing collections during probate, the legal process that sorts out someone's possessions and finances after they die. He goes behind closed doors and looks through people's lifetime collections of stuff—some of which they might have hidden from family and friends the entire time.

He describes a probate case he did in an ordinary-sized house that had belonged to an elderly man. The man had been quiet and mainly kept himself to himself, never inviting anyone over.

All the neighbors on the street assumed he had been living an extremely frugal life, judging by the dilapidated state of the house.

When Mark opened the door, the house inside was very dark, as if the curtains had been drawn shut for decades. He walked gingerly toward the windows, but realized with a start that it wasn't curtains covering them: It was moss. He flipped a light switch but nothing happened—the electricity had been cut off—and no water came out of the taps either. It was cold too. Part of the roof had fallen in a while ago, and the owner had never bothered to fix it.

Mark pulled his phone out of his pocket and took a series of flash photos to catch glimpses of the contents of the house, as this was before iPhones had a flashlight feature. The quick snatches he saw in the camera's flash were far from what he expected. This dark, disintegrating house, which had been overtaken by plants like Sleeping Beauty's palace, was a trove of treasures.

There was a painting by a well-known artist, fine furniture, and a clock worth around £20,000 (over $25,000). All in all, there was roughly half a million pounds' (around $630,000) worth of antiques in the tumbledown house.

This lonesome owner had been a serious antiques collector, to the detriment of the other parts of his life. He had spent his money on buying furniture and paintings while he sat shivering from the cold and eating a monk's diet.

"The antiques owned him," says Mark. "He couldn't leave them, and it's like: Why would you live a life like that? He was living in complete squalor."

Why We Collect: The Thrill of the Chase

Later in my visit, Mark showed me around the huge warehouse rooms where they store all the art and furniture before it gets sold. In one room, a workman was grappling with an oil painting that must have been about six-and-a-half feet long, trying to wrap it in brown paper to send to its new owner. In another, there were a huge number of cabinets that stored row after row of china figurines. Jewelry was everywhere. I edged around gingerly, lifting my arms up high, desperately trying not to break anything and so leave with a five-figure bill.

Seeing that much stuff at once felt a little overwhelming, and I was surprised to find that Mark had felt something similar in the past.

He was originally drawn to his career through a passion for collecting that started when he was a child. It began with a particular kind of china that he loved, and over time he taught himself everything about it. It was a rare type, which made it more difficult to collect: Finding a new piece might take months of going to fairs and searching online.

To begin with, the aim was to "complete" his collection by buying every single piece possible in order to create a full "set." But one event dramatically changed his mind, after he was invited to an auction of a fellow enthusiast's lifetime collection—something that, on the surface, he should have loved as an ideal opportunity to pick up several pieces that he was missing.

All the china was laid out in one room of the auction house, and champagne was passed around for potential buyers as they browsed. Mark walked into the room, then walked straight back out again. "I was looking at my future, and I didn't want it," says Mark. "That was his whole life; he would leave business trips [to buy china], leave his wife on holiday."

Collecting is all about the chase, says Mark. This man had spent his life traveling the world, scouring the internet, and reading collectors' magazines, hoping to hear of a sighting of a new piece, like it was an endangered species that he was hunting down. While some collectors are motivated by pure passion for a type of object, others treat it as a sport. And the thrill of the chase simply wasn't enough for Mark.

Dr. Shirley Mueller has a very unusual way of seeing the collecting world. She has had two completely different careers, first as a neurologist—a doctor who treats the brain and nervous system—and then as an expert in and collector of Chinese porcelain. On a scientific level, she can tell you exactly which chemicals in which specific part of the brain give her the thrill of buying a new teapot for her collection. But that doesn't stop her enjoying it. In 2019 she published *Inside the Head of a Collector*, a book about her unique perspective on the art world.[1] I speak to her from her home in Indianapolis, where she displays a small selection of the 560 or so pieces in her collection (the vast majority of it is packed away in storage). I ask whether collecting is for her more about the hunting of objects, or about having and appreciating them once you've bought them.

Without missing a beat, she says, "The hunting."

She explains her answer in two ways, starting with the science. As you may know, things often seem a lot more exciting before you buy them than they do when you own them. Art collectors go mad trying to buy a particular painting, then put it in storage and forget about it. Clothes look much better when you're trying them on than they do once you own them. People ruin their lives for the thrill of an affair. Think back to chapter one, when we talked about the incredibly powerful effects of dopamine, the neurotransmitter that is closely involved in feelings of motivation.

"Our pleasure center, the nucleus accumbens, is stimulated more by anticipation of getting what we want than actually getting it," says Dr. Mueller. "So the hunt is the really exciting part, and then when a collector gets what they're looking for, and it's on their shelf, it's largely forgotten. Then it's on to the next thing."

As we saw, from an evolutionary perspective this makes a lot of sense. If humans were overwhelmed with lasting joy when they got the food or shelter they wanted, they would rest on their laurels instead of getting up and finding their next meal. The same wiring is used when collectors are finding their next purchase, says Dr. Mueller. She points to the story of Claribel Cone, who together with her sister Etta became one of the most important collectors of modern art in the nineteenth and twentieth centuries, as they amassed three thousand works by contemporary artists, including Matisse, Gauguin, and Picasso. There was no way that all of this could be displayed at once in their apartments (the collection now takes up an entire wing of the Baltimore Museum of Art). But they kept on buying regardless, with Claribel even buying a piece on her deathbed. "[Collectors] don't stop," says Dr. Mueller. "It's not uncommon for collectors to purchase very, very near to the end of their life."

Dr. Mueller can describe the neuroscience behind all the curious ways that collectors act. But unusually for an academic expert, many of whom look at their subject with the objectivity of distance, she also gets it. She, too, feels the drive to hunt and collect.

Until recently, her collection was around twice as big. As well as being in storage, it was all over her house. Her husband's wardrobe stored china instead of clothes, and they couldn't use their dining table for eight years because of the three-foot-tall porcelain cistern on top of it, which was so precious they needed to hire an expert to move it.

Because of these space issues, Dr. Mueller decided to sell off much of her collection, including some of her best pieces, in an online auction run by Christie's. The porcelain she sold included a pair of blue foot-high jars from the seventeenth century for $30,000, and a pair of brightly colored decorative roosters that had once belonged to J. P. Morgan for $20,000.

Despite what might seem like extraordinary prices to an outsider, Dr. Mueller was a little disappointed with the results. Although she made money from the sales, she thinks she would have made two or three times more at better times in the market. After all the effort she had put into creating her collection, the relatively low prices felt personal. It was like "I [was] allowing myself to be exhibited, as my porcelains are a reflection of my very being," she wrote in *Fine Art Connoisseur* magazine.[2] She had to reassure herself that "'this is OK; my porcelains are desirable,' which by inference made me desirable as well, since I had selected them."

If you're not from the serious collecting world, it might seem strange to spend so much time, effort, and money searching for and buying these particular objects, only to put them away in storage. It reminds me of crabbing on family vacations when I was a child. You spend a few hours waiting for crabs to nibble on your line, then you reel them in and put them in a bucket. We never ate them, so at the end of the afternoon we simply released them back into the sea and watched them scurry off. Crabbing isn't about finding a delicious dinner for that evening; it's a way to spend an afternoon sitting and chatting with the people you care about.

This can be a good way to think about the motivations of collectors, says Dr. Mueller. Collectors often don't see themselves as owners of things, but more like the temporary custodians of historically important objects who keep them safe for the next generation. When they're finished, they release them back into the wild—which in this case means through selling or donating to museums.

The time you spend on your collection is the joy of it, she says. It would be easy to look at the enormous sums involved and think it a lot of money for inanimate objects that are kept in storage. Couldn't the money be better spent in bringing you joy in the way that experiences such as a vacation with loved ones would?

But collecting is spending on an experience, says Dr. Mueller, and it comes with the added benefit of a souvenir at the end. "The collector has experiences, [but] also has something to show that is concrete at the end. "For [other] experiences, you have to have pictures to show people."

Why We Collect: Passion and Interest

In my conversations with collectors, I realized that all of them had told me versions of the same story. As a child, or a teenager, they had seen something that had completely captured their attention and showed them how different their life could be.

In Mark's case, he was only eight when porcelain caught his eye and suggested a life beyond the rough and tumble of the playground. Dr. Mueller was a teenager when she saw a film set in 1930s China, and she was transfixed by the country and the historical setting, an experience that later pushed her toward a love of antique Chinese porcelain. These experiences, at young and impressionable ages, sparked passions for certain objects and what they represent.

This straightforward interest for the objects might put Mark and Dr. Mueller into the "pure collector" category, as set out in a 2021 study by a group of European business and finance researchers, who looked at the personality traits of collectors.[3]

They used the Big Five test, one of the most common ways in psychology to categorize personality, which sorts different traits into five groups, then gives a percentage score for each. The categories are openness to experience (trying new things or following a tried-and-true route); conscientiousness (organized and detail-focused or careless and spontaneous); extroversion (gregarious or preferring alone time); agreeableness (empathetic and people-pleasing or critical); and neuroticism (worried and anxious or confident). The traits can be remembered by their acronym: OCEAN or CANOE. (You may wish to discover your own Big Five personality traits with a test online.)

Using a survey of over four thousand people, the authors of this study looked at how the personalities of collectors compared to those of non-collectors. In general, collectors tended to score more highly than average on openness, while scoring low on neuroticism—by and large, they are a curious and confident group of people.

The research then broke collectors down into subgroups, depending on their reasons for collecting. The personalities of consumption-focused collectors were similar to non-collectors, but a little more open. Those who collected for investment tended to have lower levels of agreeableness and conscientiousness, "which relates to a competitive and spontaneous personality," wrote the authors. The final group, "pure collectors," those who collect for the love of it, showed high levels of openness and conscientiousness—they are interested in the world, but also have a level of focus and reliability that keeps them on course for a long time.

Of course, it wasn't just personality that made a difference. The study found that collectors tended to be more financially comfortable and highly educated than the wider population.

"Healthy" and "Unhealthy" Collecting

One day at work I was procrastinating by scrolling through social media when I saw a Zillow listing for a house that had gone viral. On a tucked-away hill sat a three-bedroom house, which initially looked pretty ordinary: beige carpets, white walls, and a pale-wood kitchen. But after taking a turn off the kitchen, the strangeness began. Room after room appeared to exist only to store things—with a mixture of floor-to-ceiling shelves and built-in locked cabinets. Off the main house, just beyond all these storage rooms, was what could only be described as a personal warehouse. It had a floor space of 2,400 square feet (which is three-and-a-half times the size of my entire flat), a sixteen-foot high ceiling, and walls lined with hundreds of shelves—every single one of them completely empty. My brain couldn't look at the pictures and make sense of it as part of a house rather than an Amazon warehouse or the storage room of a museum. Just . . . what on earth do you need all that space for?

The *New York Post* asked the estate agents and found out that the house had been owned by an eighty-nine-year-old woman who had owned over twenty-five thousand books, as well as thousands of DVDs, video tapes, and pieces of memorabilia.[4] The warehouse room was never completely full but had been built with enough space to allow for future shopping.

I clicked through the comments on the story. People were baffled. They thought that perhaps the owner of the house was crazy, either a doomsday prepper or cult leader. No one in their right mind would need that much storage.

But is this true? Is there anything necessarily wrong with collecting a lot if it brings you a huge amount of joy and doesn't have any adverse effect on your life or on that of others?

Psychologists who research collecting have tried a few times to define what counts as "healthy" or "normal." A 2005 paper from the University of Iowa set out several criteria to distinguish "normal" from "abnormal" as they looked into how brain injuries in some people can lead to collecting.[5]

The line between these two categories is relatively fine and depends a lot on subjective interpretation. The researchers consider whether the collecting began after the injury, as well as asking whether the subject has an "excessive" number of things compared to "normal behavior," and in the context of their living situation; whether the items themselves are of "little or no value"; if the collecting gets in the way of daily life; and if the habit lasts for a year or more and continues even after attempts to stop.

But words like excessive, normal, and little or no value mean different things to different people. Even the authors' definition of a collection feels extremely subjective, being defined as "the accumulation of any type of object in a greater number than is considered reasonable by peers and is thus noted as 'unusual' or 'remarkable.'" I find it "unusual" and "remarkable" when people own more than two lipsticks, while my very glamorous girlfriends think that having enough products to fill a small chest of drawers is normal.

Hoarding

When Megan Karnes arrived in the United Kingdom in 1997, British culture was a bit of a shock. American-born and -bred, she had pursued a career in show business, which made landing in buttoned-up, reserved Britain jarring. What she found particularly odd was the British stiff-upper-lip approach to dealing with difficult feelings, which was worlds away from the openness she saw in the United States.

She thought that Brits could benefit from her approach, so she decided to change careers and work in mental health. Her first post was with a mental health charity that focused on obsessive compulsive disorder (OCD). At the time, hoarding was seen as a symptom of OCD rather than its own condition, but over the years, Karnes saw that there was an enormous demand from people who needed to have hoarding treated as a primary concern.

She heard story after story from people who were struggling with the effect that hoarding was having on their lives. One man slept in his car because his house had become too cluttered to live in. Another worked with Karnes for fourteen weeks before he felt able to put a single newspaper in the recycling bin. A woman found it nearly impossible to throw away a rotting egg.

★ ★ ★

Over time, the psychology establishment caught up with people's on-the-ground experiences of hoarding, and in 2012 it was classified as a condition of its own. It is more common than you might think, with 2.6 percent of the population having it, according to the American Psychological Association.[6]

The boundary between what counts as hoarding disorder and what is just problematic collecting can be a little subjective, but the National Health Service (NHS) says that it depends on how people organize their things.[7] It says that a hoard is "usually very disorganized, takes up a lot of room and the items are largely inaccessible," while a collection is the opposite. As an example, according to the NHS, someone who collects newspaper reviews might cut out reviews and put them in scrapbooks, while a hoarder might keep whole newspapers that "clutter their entire house" and make it difficult to find the right review. Intriguingly, it adds that hoarding doesn't exist just in the physical world. You can hoard data, too, if you hold on to "huge amounts" of virtual files, documents, or emails and are "extremely reluctant" to delete them.

Professor Gail Steketee, a professor emerita at Boston University who spent her career studying hoarding and OCD, pioneered a test called the Saving Inventory, which can be used to measure someone's hoarding and collecting habits.[8] It splits hoarding into three areas: the extent of clutter, how difficult it is to throw things away, and what someone's habits are around acquiring new things. The quantity of things you have is just one element of diagnosis; also included on the scale are the feelings that someone might experience about their possessions, and how they are affecting their life. If you are interested, you can take the test at home.

It's quite likely that, up until now, most of what you've gleaned about people who hoard is from watching TV programs made about them for entertainment. Typically, these shows work in a similar way: They start by showing an extremely full and cluttered home and dwell on the potential dangers of living there. Next, they move on to the person who hoards, who explains their completely unique way of seeing their possessions, one that their family finds difficult and exasperating. After that, a professional organizer comes in, throws away most of their things, and cleans the house. And then—hey presto!—the happy family wanders round their newly tidied house in awe of the progress that's been made and thank the TV crew as they head home.

It's not surprising that people who hoard, and those who work with them, have a complicated relationship with these documentaries. Although they can be effective at raising awareness of the condition, they also push the idea that recovery is achieved through what you can see on-screen—turning a cluttered home into a tidy one. Job done. Or is it?

"We don't go to a person who's dealing with alcoholism, pick up the bottle of vodka, crush it on the floor, and say "Don't you feel better now?" says Karnes. She argues that hoarding, like alcoholism or addictions, is not a "lifestyle choice"—it's a compulsion driven by complex psychological factors.

What Causes Hoarding?

The reasons why someone might develop hoarding are numerous, but research has shown that there are a few factors that can increase the risk. One of the most common is having an experience of trauma or loss, particularly in your early life.

Sometimes it can be easy to draw a line from past experience to future behavior, as in the case of a woman whom Professor Steketee worked with who obsessively collected Barbie dolls in their original boxes. After asking her about her early childhood, some of the causes of this behavior became clear. As a child, the woman had built up a small collection of dolls. One summer she went away on vacation and came home to find that her grandmother had given them all away. While this wasn't the only factor that led to her later hoarding, it had to have something to do with it, says Steketee.

This story felt a little familiar to me—in one moment, this little girl's understanding of the world dramatically shifted. Before, she thought the world was safe and predictable, the kind of place where you can trust that your beloved things will still be there when you get home. But this shock had huge consequences on her worldview. She learned that the world is not predictable; sometimes bad things happen with no warning, and there is nothing you can do about it.

But sometimes the traumatic events that trigger hoarding do not have an obvious link to our possessions. For example, Professor Steketee worked with someone else who had been the victim of sexual violence in her home. This had clearly had a profound impact on her mental health, and her sense of safety, even within her own home, had been completely shaken. In response, she started to hoard, a part of her believing that if her home were very cluttered with possessions then it would be harder for an intruder to get in. Her things were not just things to her—they were a desperate attempt to keep herself safe.

It is not just emotional trauma that can trigger hoarding. Sometimes cognitive factors are involved too. Researchers have found that difficulties with sorting and categorizing objects can feed into hoarding, as people find it more difficult to work out how to store things and keep them tidy. A piece of 2006 research from Harvard found that this can exist in people who do not have a clinical diagnosis as hoarders but would still consider themselves "packrats."[9]

The authors took forty-one people and presented them, one by one, with twenty random objects, including "an upbeat fortune from a fortune cookie," two stamps, an old magazine, a chocolate bar, a die, and a button. They asked them to sort these objects into categories—but how they did so was up to them. They could choose two or twenty categories, and sort them by anything from color to function to monetary value.

The packrats found this task "significantly more stressful and difficult" than the control group did and took longer to complete it. Interestingly, they also decided to sort the things into more categories than the other group did, something that the researchers called underinclusiveness. Instead of being able to quickly and decisively put things into broad categories like "edible vs. nonedible" or "things to trash vs. Things to keep," they saw more nuances and quirks in each individual thing, meaning that more categories were required. The authors write that the collectors seemed to see "the uniqueness of each object, making it difficult for them to categorize." It's easy to see how this could make someone much more likely to hoard: If every object feels like it's unique and special, why wouldn't you hold on to it?

A related element to hoarding is someone's ability to make rules, says Steketee. You might not realize it, but most of us follow a set of subconscious rules to make decisions about which objects to buy and which to throw away. My rules include the following: Ignore best-before dates on food, but get rid of anything that smells bad; don't buy shoes that aren't comfortable, even if they're on sale; socks with holes larger than a nickel are immediately thrown away. Your rules will probably be completely different from mine, but it's likely that you do have them even if you aren't aware of it. These rules are helpful, says Steketee, because they allow us to make quick decisions. I do not have to consider the pros and cons of keeping every individual holey sock: Once it's past the threshold I've set, it's gone.

But if you see each object as unique, as we saw in the research above, then you might find it harder to create a set of generalized rules that apply to different sorts of objects. Doing spring-cleaning can be overwhelming given the thousands of individual decisions you have to make. A set of premade rules makes it much faster.

Karnes says that hoarding for some people can also be connected to perfectionism or a desire to be "good." Perhaps this seems counterintuitive, as having a lot of clutter is not a perfect outcome.

An example of this would be the woman mentioned earlier who refused to let go of her rotten egg. Despite knowing the egg could have no possible use, the feelings that it set off for her stopped her from throwing it away. "She kept the egg because she didn't want to waste it," says Karnes. "[It's thinking] 'I have to be totally good; I cannot waste.'" She wanted so badly to not waste the egg; to be a "good" person who doesn't waste food. Throwing away the egg would show that she had made a mistake in the past by not eating it quickly enough.

★ ★ ★

Collecting and hoarding can be the cause or effect of either pleasure or deep distress.

Hearing Shirley Mueller describe her life of collecting made that clear to me. While I initially couldn't understand why anyone would put so much time and money into buying things just to have them sit in boxes in a cupboard, it made sense after she reframed her collecting as a global treasure hunt that allowed her to explore her passions and make friends. As she said, collecting is first and foremost a rewarding hobby—albeit one that comes with souvenirs.

Collecting isn't like that for everyone, though. It can feel like a burden or a duty—or even become a compulsion that requires medical intervention to solve. Think of Mark the auctioneer, who felt that he owed it to his collection to keep going once he'd started, until he woke up to the fact that he didn't want to devote his life to it.

The first type of collecting might be worthwhile, while the second definitely isn't. Collect if you enjoy it; don't if you don't. If you have a half-formed collection that you feel is weighing you down, sell or donate it. Not only will you be making yourself a lot happier, but by releasing your collection back into the wild, you'll be allowing a passionate collector the joy of hunting it down.

FINAL THOUGHTS

WHAT ARE YOUR RULES?

In this chapter we saw how following a set of rules for buying and keeping stuff is much easier than making individual decisions in the moment. Think through the rules you have set yourself, which you might have done subconsciously. When, or under what circumstances, do you decide that it's time to buy more food, toiletries, clothing, or books? When, or under what circumstances, do you decide that it's time to get rid of those things?

CLARIFY

Consider how straightforward these rules are. A clear rule around buying would be "I buy new socks when I have fewer than five good pairs left." A complex one would be "I buy new socks when I need them, or when I see a 'good' offer, or a pattern that I like, or if I see a pair that reminds me of ones that I used to have." Clear rules make it much easier to make shopping decisions that are in your long-term interest.

Do the same for your rules around discarding. An example of a clear rule here might be "I donate all clothes that no longer fit me," while a complicated one would be "If an item of clothing doesn't fit me, I take into account its condition, how long ago I bought it, the memories I created while wearing it, and the last time I wore it to decide whether to keep or donate it." Clear rules make it much quicker to decide what to do with your belongings—allowing you to part with things with less upset. Could you make rules that are clearer?

WHY ARE YOU COLLECTING?

Collections can cost a lot of money, time, and effort. They can also create a sense of obligation: Once they've been started, they have to be kept going. But you really don't have to. Your collection doesn't have feelings; you don't owe it anything. It won't be upset if you get rid of it.

To test your feelings of duty or obligation, ask yourself a few questions:

- Think of the first item that started it off—did you choose it yourself, or were you given it?
- Did you consciously set out to build a collection, or did it turn into one over time?
- Do you feel a sense of obligation to buy a new item for your collection when you see one for sale?
- If you started a collection from scratch today, is this what you would choose?
- Does your collection offer other benefits, like connection to a community of other enthusiasts?
- Do you actively enjoy searching for new additions to your collection?
- If your entire collection were somehow lost, would you start it from scratch?

How do your collected items fit into your life? Collections of any type can cost us by taking up space in our homes that we could otherwise live in. On Professor Steketee's Saving Inventory, there are several questions that probe into how the things we own impact our ability to use and enjoy our homes. She asks people to consider both the material extent of their possessions, like whether they can use their homes fully, and the emotional impact that being in that space has on them.

How does it feel to ask those questions? Do your collections justify the mental and physical space that you devote to them?

You Can't Hold On
to Every Memory

I t was one of those storage boxes you get in a craft shop. It
cost about four pounds and was nothing more than a pretty
shoebox: glossy, deep purple cardboard, corners reinforced with
metal and a little slot into which you could put a label. The lid
hovered on top, never quite closing because it was so full.

It was home to a selection of things: mostly stuff that I didn't
quite need but couldn't bear to throw away. Ticket stubs, boarding
passes, Polaroids of friends, postcards from my parents. Love letters from exes, notes from my late uncle. Invitations to weddings,
menus from big parties, matchboxes from smart hotels. Anything
that reminded me of a time I never wanted to forget.

To someone else, it would have looked like the contents of
a garbage bin. But to me, it was everything: all the most special
memories of my life in one place. I saw it as a kind of USB stick

for my brain: a store of my memories, out in the world, because I couldn't hold them all in my head. I could just pick up that old postcard and *whoosh*, memories of that girls' trip to France come back so clearly that I can feel the hot tiles under my feet. Going through the junk in that box reminded me of every person I had ever been: the brazen child, the boy-band fangirl, the lover, the writer, the friend.

The contents of the box were always growing and changing, but it held a constant role in my life. I turned to it when I was lost. Without it, I needed a new map.

★ ★ ★

One rainy weekend I was in the National Gallery in London with my sister, Rosie, on a tour of the Renaissance galleries. We tried to keep to the front of the group, trotting after the guide as she went from one painting to the next, racing to get a spot on one of the hard benches and rest our feet.

The last stop was *Venus and Mars* by Botticelli. It is a wide and short painting, the shape of an envelope, with Venus, the goddess of love and sex, and Mars, the god of war, reclining across it. They are painted like marble sculptures, their luminous flesh partly veiled by flowing fabric. Venus is propped up, looking dignified and calm as she gazes across the canvas to Mars, who is fast asleep with his head dropping backward. You could see it as a feminist statement, a joke about men falling asleep after sex, or a comment about love triumphing over war.

I stared and stared at it: I loved the joyous oranges and pinks and the playful tone of the whole piece. It felt so sunny and hopeful, which made the guide's little speech all the more depressing.

"For a painting dated from 1485, the brightness of the colors is extraordinary," she said. "We can thank prudent conservation for extending its life, but just like us, no painting will last forever. It is disintegrating every day, and having it out on display under the lights makes it fade even faster. If we kept it in a temperature-controlled vault we could add another few years onto its life, but we have to accept it—nothing lasts forever, and one day this will be dust."

Rosie and I looked at each other and raised our eyebrows.

What a miserable thing to say!

I looked away from my sister and back to the guide, whose serene face was turned toward the painting. I couldn't make sense of it; what she said had sounded so gloomy, and yet she clearly didn't see it that way. It felt as if the eventual end date on the painting made her appreciate its current presence all the more, rather than worrying about it falling apart in the future.

Afterward, at lunch, Rosie and I talked it over, trying to work it out. "I guess you can never look after something literally forever," she said. "It just seems like forever to us, if something is already five hundred years old and will go on for another few hundred or whatever."

I nodded. "Yeah, I agree. I just sort of wish she hadn't said it out loud."

She nodded. We have similar personalities, both of us prone to sentimentality and romanticizing the past. Even though we are now very much grown up, we strictly police all our family traditions, making sure that every birthday or Christmas is just as it has always been. We have always sensed the fact that life is nothing but constant change, and that growing up is nothing more than a series of farewells to the things you love.

One summer when we were teenagers, we decided to try to stop this for a moment by making a time capsule. We filled a shoebox with mementos and things that we thought captured the present moment, along with letters to our future selves, then scrawled warnings over it saying it could not be opened for ten years. Burying it in the garden seemed like too much effort, so we stowed it in the cupboard under the stairs.

Over the next decade, it felt like we were leaving the capsule to brew, letting its poignancy grow and deepen over time, allowing a little mystery around it to develop.

By the time we opened it, we had almost forgotten what we had put in. There was a copy of the local newspaper, which if it hadn't been faded and yellowed could have been from that week—garbage collections are always big news, apparently. There were a couple of magazines and a few CDs, which by that point we didn't use any more. Oddly, we had also each put in a school report, but most interesting of all were the letters we'd written to our future selves. I don't know what Rosie's said, as she would only let me read tiny snippets of it (make of that what you will), but mine was four pieces of paper torn from a notebook then written on both sides and jammed into a too-small envelope. The intervening period had been so long, and of such formative years, that I barely recognized the handwriting as my own. What had by adulthood developed into an upright cursive had begun as a rounded and cramped script, giving the impression of a hand struggling to keep up with a frantic mind. I had made a list of aspirations for life in my midtwenties, which included "living in a flat in London," being a journalist," and "being married, or at the very LEAST engaged." I would have made my teenage self very proud on the first two, but I cackled at the last one.

Opening the time capsule made me think again about the purple box, which in many ways served the same purpose. Both were ways to pour the liquid past into a container, trying to stop it from running away.

But the fire had claimed the purple box, and my other things too. Had my memories gone as well?

While I was thinking about ways to refurnish the new flat, I would look up minimalist blogs on the internet, which would say things like "Memories are all in your head! You don't need to keep so much stuff!" Well, you must be a genius then, I'd think. Although I will remember the big, important episodes, there is no way I can remember all the small, daily details of life in the past without my things. Photos stop all New Year's Eve parties from merging into one. The stained pages of cookbooks are like journals, marking out when you shared warm dinners with friends.

It felt like there was an impending deadline. For the time being, I would be able to remember a number of tender and lovely moments. But my memories were all I had to rely on, and as time went on, they would fade. The most important moments would remain, while others would disappear entirely.

The long process of forgetting started much sooner than I expected. One night, friends from university came over to see the new flat. We got onto one of our favorite conversations: gossiping about what the other people in our year were doing now. I felt an urge to go and grab that purple box and pass around the pictures of our old sports teams and nights out, but I couldn't. Instead, I was quiet for a while, trying to remember the name of that girl who used to live down the road from us. Was it Lucy, or Louise? I didn't know.

It felt like being in the woods at dusk: You can still see the trees, but you know that darkness is coming soon. I wondered whether there might be a flashlight to light the way.

★ ★ ★

Another few months later and it was Christmas, almost a year on from the fire. The year was coming to an end, and it felt like some of my sadness was too. I was still grieving my relationship and my stuff, but I was certain that even if things weren't yet getting better, they had stopped getting worse.

In that slack time while I was waiting for the new year I decided to sort out my photos, which were spread over two different cloud platforms, a hard drive, and two phones. It took a full day to download, sort, and re-upload everything, but I found the overheating laptop on my knees comforting.

I had lost so many memories with the fire, but I found plenty of them again in these photos. Between them, my parents probably have a thousand photographs that cover their entire lives from birth to age forty-five, when digital cameras came in. In my cloud storage, I have a thousand photos from 2019 alone. What a gift it is to be able to waste photographs on cloudy skies and fresh haircuts.

Instead of doing what I would usually do—dumping all the photos into one big messy folder where I would never find them again—I wanted to be prudent and make sure that there was a way I could access and enjoy this great number of images. It was too much to look through every single one and decide if each was worth keeping, so I decided to go halfway, and bundle them into folders by year.

So many of my pictures recorded those straightforwardly happy times. Getting ready on the morning of a friend's wedding, three matching bridesmaid's dresses hanging from a door. Various combinations of friends on different beaches around Europe. Sitting in restaurants late at night. Glasses of wine, bottles of peach iced tea. Candles burned halfway down on birthday cakes.

There were other times, too, difficult times that I had misremembered, forgetting the whispers of pleasure that were there even on the grayest of days. The months after the fire were miserable, but look: There I was, sitting on a friend's sofa, laughing. And there again, my sister with her mouth slung open, pointing to a fish the size of a toddler in a restaurant. Those days weren't the biggest, most special days of my life, but they were nice. The smoldering, warm glow of normal life.

Between these small joys was a lot of mundanity that I had forgotten about. Hard-boiled eggs, journeys on the bus; these quotidian moments must have been worth capturing at the time, but I couldn't now remember why.

I stopped for a minute on a photo like that, from earlier that year. The time stamp showed it was taken the morning after my first night staying in the new flat, six months on from the fire. It shows my new bedroom: In the foreground is my pillow and a corner of my mussed-up duvet, and behind the bed is the window. The image has a warm, pink light from the morning sun coming through my new curtains, which are roughly pulled back. It looks like I took the picture lying in bed, pointing the camera upward, toward the bright blue sky. It was a completely average scene, but one that I found mysteriously beautiful.

When All Your Memories Are Lost

Before 2018, the town of Paradise, California, lived up to its name. It was a small town with a strong community set in the foothills of the Sierra Nevada mountains and surrounded by thickets of pine trees.

Things changed in the early hours of November 8, 2018, when a faulty power line caused a spark and set Paradise on fire. Strong winds fanned the flames across the parched, rain-starved land, and the fire spread rapidly. Within a few hours there was so much smoke and ash in the sky that it was dark, like night had fallen. People raced to escape the town, causing jams on the roads out. Some who couldn't escape in time sought shelter, fleeing to the last remaining places in town that weren't on fire: parking lots, an antique shop, a lake. The scale of the blaze is difficult to comprehend. On the first day of the fire, it destroyed nearly 50 acres every minute. In total, 52,000 people were evacuated and tragically, 85 people died. Over 95 percent of buildings in Paradise were destroyed, taking with them the homes and worldly possessions of thousands of people and causing damage mounting to $16.65 billion.

Isabelle Kennedy is a sociology researcher at Boston College in Massachusetts who spent months interviewing victims of the fire, asking them how the loss of their homes and possessions has affected their lives. On her visits in the aftermath of the fire, it was like walking on another planet, she said. The ground was raw and orange, and the fire had been so huge and hot that things that you would never expect had burnt. Toilets had exploded into ash, metal had melted. The railings at the side of the roads were gone, the tarmac on the streets was pocked and burnt. "I was there midway through the cleanup," she says. "Half the [house] lots were piles of rubble and ash, and the other half of lots were cleared and just flat." In general the people of Paradise fell into three categories after they lost their stuff, says Kennedy. The first group used their insurance payouts to try to replace everything exactly as it was. "One person was like: 'We immediately went online to eBay and found this cuckoo clock that someone gave us for our wedding,'" she says. "In their minds it's the same: They still have it, they didn't lose it, and it still has that personal significance." The second group were deeply unsettled by the financial losses they suffered and responded by collecting as many things as they could. They would come to the donation centers set up for victims and leave with "everything they could possibly find," says Kennedy. The third group did something quite different. They embraced a minimalist lifestyle, replacing the basics and almost nothing else. Even where they could buy facsimiles of the things they had before, they didn't; it never felt the same without the memories attached. "We collect things because they remind us who we are," says Kennedy. The move towards minimalism for those people was therefore part of "a trauma response . . . all of a sudden after losing [their things] in a fire, [they] feel very vulnerable," says Kennedy. "They don't feel like a secure place to put your identity." After these people's homes had burnt down, it was as if they needed another place to put all that care and all those memories. As a result, many became attached to the piles of ash that remained on the lots where their houses had been. Even though almost no discernible objects were left, these people were heartbroken when their particular piles of ash were cleared away. "It was the only proof that they had of the life they'd lived," says Kennedy.

How Memory Works

We've all felt it at some point: Maybe it's been years since your first job, but after stumbling on an old pencil skirt at the back of your wardrobe, memories of it seem clear as day. It can feel like our brains actually need physical objects to remember the past, especially moments that were a long time ago. Why is this? I decided to get to the bottom of it, starting with understanding how our memories work on a microscopic level.

The brain is composed of neurons, which are specialized cells that look a little like a tree: long and thin in the middle, with branches poking up at the top and roots at the bottom. These roots and branches make them very good at attaching to one another and forming complex networks across the brain.

Individual neurons tend to fire only in response to very selective stimuli. Well-known research from the California Institute of Technology published in 2005 studied the minds of eight people with epilepsy who had had one hundred tiny electrodes inserted in their brains as part of treatment for their seizures.[1] Researchers showed the patients pictures of various celebrities, as well as images of their names written down, and used the electrodes to measure how their brains responded.

One woman tested had a "Jennifer Aniston neuron": a cell that responded every time she was shown a picture of the actress or read her name written down. Another woman on the trial had a Halle Berry neuron, which performed a similar role. Perhaps as you are reading this sentence, your very own Halle Berry neuron is firing up.

To create complex memories, your brain connects neurons from across the brain to bring together different types of information. When you want to recall something, the "librarian" of your brain—your hippocampus, a curved structure tucked deep into the middle of your skull—helps to find different details and stitch them all together. If you are at trivia and are asked about the cast of *Friends*, your hippocampus will dig through your brain's filing system and find your Jennifer Aniston neuron and your David Schwimmer neuron.

As we learn and go over a piece of information, or practice a skill, the neurons responsible for remembering it will strengthen the connections between them. To our conscious minds, this will feel like the memory is easier to call up.

Think of when you first started your job. You might have remembered your colleagues' names by associating them with where in the office they sat: Alex by the elevator doors, Charlotte in the corner. But after a year at the company you might be able to remember their names easily when they pass you in the corridor, with no prompts needed. The neurons responsible have strengthened their connections, and you no longer need extra help.

The opposite is true with memories you don't often recall. The connections between neurons are weak, and to retrieve the memory you might need one or more cues.

You may have experienced the phenomenon that occurs after desperately cramming in the days before (or, in my case, even the hours before) an exam at school or university. Although you might be able to recall the necessary facts in the exam, you might forget everything quickly afterward. In your day-to-day life you don't need to know about the solar system or *The Odyssey*, so your knowledge of those topics will dissolve over time as their neuronal networks are neglected.

Researchers divide memories into two categories depending on their strength. The first are recall memories: strong ones you can bring to mind at will with no or very few cues, such as your date of birth. The second type are recognition-only: memories that are so weak that, while you can't recall them offhand, they have just enough presence in your mind that you could confirm them if the information is offered to you.

Maybe you can't remember the name of an old neighbor, although it feels like it's on the tip of your tongue. But if someone said "Anna," it would feel like you had suddenly remembered it, and you would be able to confidently say that it was correct. This is a recognition-level memory.

In the middle is a gray area where you could remember a fact under the right circumstances and with a lot of prompts. It's almost like our brains use the external world as a source of extra storage. As time goes on, memories are condensed and the details are lost, so it's only when you go back to your university town or see a picture of yourself in that old dress that you can once again access those memories.

I waited out the worst of the 2020 pandemic with my family, in the town where I grew up. A few months in, desperate for a bit of novelty, I decided to extend my daily walk to go past the first house I had ever lived in, which we moved out of when I was seven. Although I desperately missed that home in the year or so after we moved, in my adult life I have thought about it only a handful of times. If I ever tried to conjure up an image of it, I would be able to recall just a few basics, like the red brick walls or the ballerina wallpaper I had in my bedroom.

But on the sunny day when I passed by, it felt like the last few decades hadn't happened. I stood for a moment and looked at the house, and a wash of tiny details came over me. I could suddenly remember the time I slipped on the stairs; the ivy-patterned bedspread in my parents' room; how scared I was of the dark garage.

Weaker memories are like locked doors: You need a key to open them. And often, physical objects are the key.

The Longer You've Owned Something, the Harder It Is to Throw Away

There is another way of seeing the relationship between our stuff and our memories, if we can consider not just the neuroscience but the behavior that it gives rise to. A field called behavioral economics studies the weirdness of how humans buy and keep objects, and many of its findings feel spookily close to home.

Let's start with a thought experiment. Imagine you went to a concert in 2010 with your two best friends at the time. The night was nothing special, but a perfectly nice time with people you like and music you tolerate.

Imagine that that night your friends persuaded you to come to the merch stand while they bought T-shirts, which were twenty-five dollars each. You dawdled at the back, waiting as they picked out their favorite designs and the best color, and eventually the seller said that if all three of you bought one, he'd do you a deal: Buy three for fifty-five dollars. You agreed.

Over the past ten years, you've put that T-shirt on when you most need comfort. It is slouchy and loose, its fabric is worn and softened, and it reminds you of the days when you had time to waste on mediocre nights out.

How much would you sell it for if someone asked? You initially didn't want it but bought it for twenty dollars, and now it's almost worn through. It should be worth next to nothing to you by now. If you wanted, you could pick up something similar in a thrift shop for three dollars. But there's almost zero chance you would take three dollars, or even the original twenty you paid for it. Most likely, someone would have to offer you much more than that for you to give it up. I have a T-shirt just like this; in fact, I have a couple of them. And yet I don't think I would sell a single one for less than sixty dollars.

Maybe I'm a bad example in this regard, but there is an element of this in all of us. It's called the endowment effect, and it's one of the best-studied concepts in behavioral science. The basic idea is that once we've owned something, it feels much more precious to us and becomes very hard to part with. You might have paid ten dollars for a mug, but once you've owned it for a year and it's become a favorite, there's no way you'd sell it to anyone for less than twenty.

★ ★ ★

Professor Owen Jones, who is both a professor of law and a professor of biological sciences at Vanderbilt University in Tennessee, has been researching the human and animal impulse to hold on to things for decades. He has used his dual specialties to research questions that were previously thought unanswerable by, for example, trialing brain scans to work out if someone committed a crime intentionally or by accident. In the past few decades, he has turned his attention to the endowment effect, performing tests on humans, chimpanzees, and orangutans to try to work out why we are so attached to the things we own. The effect is actually so important for survival that it is found in species other than humans.

In a fascinating set of research papers, Jones and a group of biologists, legal scholars, and zookeepers tested how attached different types of apes are to their possessions. The results in the human and chimpanzee trials are remarkably similar.

In 2007, Jones and his fellow researchers put thirty-three chimpanzees to the test.[2] In the first of a series of trials, they were given either a popsicle or a tube of peanut butter. When allowed to choose freely between the two snacks, 58 percent of them went for the peanut butter.

However, something interesting happened when they were randomly given one of the two snacks by the researchers. When they were given the peanut butter and the option to swap it for a popsicle, 79 percent of them stuck with what they had been given originally.

If the chimpanzees had just chosen the snack they liked best, then they would have chosen peanut butter 58 percent of the time, whether or not it already belonged to them. But something odd happened when they felt like they owned it already: It appeared to have become more valuable to them and thus more difficult to part with. This is a perfect example of the illogical endowment effect, and very similar to how it shows up in humans: We would never buy a ratty old T-shirt if we saw one in a thrift store, but the ones we have at home are incredibly precious to us.

The researchers then put the chimps through another, similar test, where the options were two types of dog toy: a rope chew or a bone chew. This time, when they were given one or the other randomly and then had the opportunity to swap, their behavior was completely different. They were more than happy to swap toys, seemingly at will. When the food options were taken off the table, they no longer got so attached to their possessions.

The researchers put together a few possible explanations for why the chimpanzees might be acting in this way, and these have significant implications for humans too. Even though some chimps wanted a popsicle but were given peanut butter, they seemed to prefer peanut butter when it was already in hand. This seemed to be a case of "one in the hand is worth two in the bush," according to the researchers, who surmised that the chimps' brains warn them against trading with others in case it goes wrong. The certainty of having something, even if it's not your absolute favorite, is better than taking the risk of trading with an untrustworthy zookeeper who might steal your snack and not complete her side of the bargain. So to make sure that we think twice before making a risky trade, our brains make us fall in love with the stuff we have—and feel awful when we try to part from it.

However, the chimps seemed much less concerned about losing the dog toys. Evolution has pushed our brains to get most attached to items that are crucial for our survival, suggested the researchers, which means that chimps are much less willing to give away peanut butter than dog toys.

Amazingly, when Professor Jones and other researchers ran similar experiments on humans, they got almost exactly the same results.[3] We rate the things we own as much more valuable than they really are, find it difficult to let go of stuff we see as ours, and are even more strongly attached to the objects that are critical for our survival.

But worry not; humans did manage to demonstrate a little more subtlety and complexity than the chimps. Instead of getting clingy just with food, there were several factors that made it particularly difficult for us to let go of our things, which include the following.

Firstly, as we have seen, people find anything that can demonstrate high status very appealing. Secondly, we find it hard to part with things that contribute to our health—which would explain why I am holding on to those resistance bands I haven't used in years.

Next, we ascribe a high value to anything that makes us sexually attractive to potential partners; maybe it's a slinky black dress or spray that helps you style your hair.

And lastly, we find anything with a high monetary value very sticky. The theory is that even if those things are valuable to us, we might want to cling to them in the hope that we could use them to trade with others in the future.

I certainly see these impulses in myself and wonder if these findings can explain some of the pain I felt after the fire. I was grieving for the things I loved, certainly, but maybe I was also experiencing this ancient instinct to guard my possessions. Maybe my brain was simply reacting to the sudden stripping away of resources that could have been helpful.

It's important to remember that all of this is subconscious. The people in Jones's studies didn't say to the researchers, "Evolution has primed me to hang on to this mug/pen/chocolate bar so I can trade it for food or shelter that my offspring and I could use in the future." They might not have known why they couldn't let go of that stuff.

The losses I had experienced in the fire were heartbreaking and financially devastating, of course, but I had also lost some things that I should have thrown out years ago. Maybe you feel the same: If you suddenly lost the contents of your cluttered shed, or the cupboard under your stairs, you might not replace them.

There was one drawer of my bedside table that I never opened because its contents made me feel ashamed. It included a rubber swimming cap I had used once on holiday, chargers for phones I didn't have any more, and a mouse pad I had once been given for free—particularly useless now that I used a laptop with no mouse. It was the random stuff that I owned without particularly liking, but I was adamant that there might be a use for it some day.

Admitting this makes me feel guilty. Owning things you don't need or like, and seeing it as a burden, is simply not possible for most people around the world now, or at any time in history. I wonder if that also complicates the problem. Throwing the stuff away means I didn't need it in the first place, and that makes me feel guilty too. Perhaps it's easier to just keep it in the drawer and tell myself that maybe I'll use it, someday.

The Pain of Remembering

While losing or letting go of memories can be distressing, on a biological level it seems that forgetting is actually a crucial process. Science suggests that "streamlining" memories—cutting out most details and retaining just the broad strokes of an event—helps our brains to learn.

For example, let's imagine you are biking to work on a sunny morning when you turn right without looking and a car almost hits you. If you remembered every detail of this incident, including the weather, the type of car that swerved to avoid you, and the street you were on, then the lessons you would learn from this incident would be limited. You would know to be more cautious *on this particular stretch of road with this particular car behind you*, but not to be more careful generally. In all likelihood, you would be in another accident very soon. But with a healthy forgetting brain, you will be able to learn far more quickly, so this theory goes. You will forget many of the details of the incident and retain just the key parts: When I turn without looking, I put myself in danger. Instead of being in accidents with every type of car in every street in your city before you learn to be a safe cyclist, you will change your ways far more quickly.

Going over unhappy or disappointing memories is also linked to depression. One study found that ruminating daily on the death of a loved one made people feel worse and experience grief for longer, compared to people who were not so focused on the memory.[4] Other research looked at young Nashville residents who lived through the disastrous 2010 floods in Tennessee and found that ruminators afterward showed more symptoms of depression.[5]

Constantly going over bad bits of the past could hold you back for a few reasons. Firstly, given that these memories are painful, the very act of remembering them is unpleasant and could worsen your mood and emotional health. Secondly, feelings of being trapped in the past can stop you from engaging in the present, making you withdrawn and less likely to take part in things that *do make you feel good*.

Nostalgia

But what about the happy memories from the past—should we be remembering all of them? It's easy to imagine situations you wish you could forget: Who wants to be thinking about that perfect holiday with your ex just after a breakup? Who wouldn't want to take the *Eternal Sunshine of the Spotless Mind* route and have a clean slate?

Thinking about this, I realized how my tried-and-true way of getting over a breakup is actually an exercise in manipulating my memories. I write a list of the worst moments in a relationship (something like, "that time he stood you up," "he cheated on you," "he was rude to your friends"), and when one of those happy and exquisitely painful memories springs to mind, I reread the list. The tears dry up pretty quickly.

But what about the straightforwardly happy memories—joyous scenes from childhood or times when life was carefree? Is it good for us to linger in nostalgia and keep the objects that bring up those happy memories for us?

There are caveats, but it seems that experts believe that there are benefits to reliving the good times. Professor Krystine Batcho, a professor of psychology at Le Moyne College in New York, is pretty much the world expert in nostalgia and why our stuff is so important for it. She developed the Nostalgia Inventory, a questionnaire that asks questions about how you see early experiences in your life and can "diagnose" you as a particularly wistful person.[6]

Professor Batcho speaks to me from her office in a conversation that lurches between being highly academic and so moving that I cry twice. Her way of thinking takes in both hard science and a sense of profound humanity and empathy that helps her to understand the emotional reasoning behind the weird decisions we make about our stuff.

She has been researching nostalgia for decades, and in recent years has come to realize how important our things are in connection to it after coming across memoirs of people who had particularly difficult experiences during the Second World War. "These three individuals were not connected to each other in any way, [but] they had some interesting little vignettes about the role that certain objects played in their ability to get through the war, and to get through recovery postwar, because they all ended up being forced out of their home country and moved to different places," she says. These little trinkets, none of them valuable or precious to anyone else, were connected with memories in their owners' lives. And for some reason, this nostalgia through objects helped them to make it through their difficult moments.

Professor Batcho says that the objects we get moony over are not always the ones you expect. They won't necessarily be things of high value. They might not even be things that you liked much in the past. But over the years, our most precious objects take on new meaning. From her research she has found that more likely than not, our treasured items remind us of one of two things: either what we were like in the past, or our connections to other people. "Sometimes [an object] is special because of what the object means to you. The other half is when it connects you to someone else," she says.

And as long as we're managing these collections reasonably, and not storing up huge quantities of things, then using objects to stir up nostalgia from time to time can, she says, be really helpful to us.

One of the key purposes of nostalgia is that it helps us to connect to others. Think of the last time you saw old friends—perhaps people you have known since school or university. My guess is that there was lots of reminiscing, thinking about happy times you shared or funny things you did together.

These memories put a smile on our faces and cause us to pull each other close for a minute or two. Remembering happy times is crucial for a fulfilling social life and helps us to form stable relationships. We can see how closely related nostalgia is to social bonding by thinking about our fondest memories. I would bet that yours, too, were times when you felt happy and connected to others.

Thinking of the happy times we shared can also be good for our well-being. People who are prone to nostalgia and who have warm memories of childhood are better at coping with stressful situations in the present according to a paper that Professor Batcho published in 2013.[7] And such people appear to use these memories in healthy ways: They are not escaping into the past when things get tough, but using their experiences of love and comfort to encourage them to turn to others for support.

Another reason why nostalgia is so helpful is a little more abstract but says a lot about what makes us human. Having things that remind us of the past gives us a sense of continuity. Life changes constantly. Friends move away, fashions change, our children grow up, our metabolisms slow down. Life will never be the same now as it was in the past.

Many of these changes are things we chose, or that we are glad happened, but that doesn't make it any easier to let go of the past. Even though we might love our partners desperately, we mourn the independence of our former single life. We might have fought hard for our careers, but miss our student days when we could sleep in until noon. We might be glad that our children are no longer waking up in the night, but wish they were still small enough to lie in our arms. To have a new phase of life we have to give up the last one. Time moves in only one direction, whether we like it or not.

When everything is constantly changing around us, it is deeply comforting to have things that stay the same. If you've lost your job and your relationship feels rocky, then pulling on your worn, soft T-shirt—the one that reminds you of that concert ten years ago—is intensely reassuring. The color may be a little faded now, but it's still the same top it always was. "The unknown is the major threat," says Batcho. "Whether the past was good or bad, it's certain, it's over now. We graduated from college, or we didn't. We overcame cancer, or we didn't. Things in the past happened, like it or not, and there's a certainty about it. That's so comforting."

★ ★ ★

Our memories cover every part of what it is to be human, from the best to the worst, from the profound to the trivial. Yet we can't control what we remember. We forget things we wish we could remember and remember things we wish we could forget.

In the middle of this are our things. They become talismans of important moments in our lives, taking on the meaning of times we never want to forget.

After learning that the best way to create unforgettable memories is to have as many new experiences as possible, I have said yes to everything from swing dancing to trampolining. My diary is scribbled over each week. It's wonderful, but it's not everything. I still think there is something special about physical mementos, which have the power to connect you not just to your own past, but also to other people's.

Sometimes I think about people who research their family histories, tracing stories about people who might look a bit like you but whose lives are unimaginably different. Piecing together a life from birth certificates and marriage records can feel incredibly remote—until you find a photograph. When you see the vitality in a smile, or a nose that looks a little like yours, you can start to imagine it. If a picture is worth a thousand words, a photo album could write a book.

While having plenty of new experiences might keep your own memories fresh, it won't help you share them with others. Mementos are a hand reaching out to someone else, pulling them through time. What could be more profoundly connecting than that?

But still, I think we should be choosy about what to keep. We don't need to keep everything. We don't need to remember everything, either—in fact, it's best if we don't.

Clinging to everything becomes unhelpful when we use it to give us a false sense of control over the passing of time. Time moves onward, always, even if we don't want it to, but the immutability of our things brings comfort by making us feel that the past is not as far away as it is. This can be bad for us if it spins us a false story about the present—that things in the past were especially good, that the present is lacking because it doesn't offer these particular joys. By dwelling on the past for too long—or by holding on to too many keepsakes—we are distracting ourselves from happiness in the present. Today's fun is tomorrow's happy memory.

FINAL THOUGHTS

WHAT ARE YOU YEARNING FOR?
Gather together half a dozen items that have particular sentimental value for you. One by one, recall the memories that are attached to each object, and be specific about it, as if you are

describing them to another person. This can be very instructive, revealing things that are especially important to you. Consider the explanations that Professor Batcho had for nostalgia—that it links you either to others, or to the person you once were. Maybe you have held on to lots of keepsakes from your university days, which were a time of self-discovery, freedom, and fun. If it's the friends you are remembering, are you still putting effort into staying in touch? Perhaps instead it's the feeling of infinite possibility and adventure that you miss—so why not try to bring some of that into your life now?

AUDIT WHAT YOU'RE HOLDING ON TO

Before the fire, I held on to nearly everything that reminded me of a particular time, or which made me feel sentimental in one way or another. I couldn't accept not being able to control the arrow of time, and that periods of my life that I'd loved were now over. Clinging to whatever I could gave me a false sense of control, as if I was pushing back against fate and proving that the past was still real—it must be, since I had all this old stuff.

Focusing on the past made me see the future as something to be feared rather than embraced.

Obviously the fire meant I had no choice about my mementos. But it also gave me a chance to start from the beginning and come up with a new way of doing things. I am now far more scrupulous about the things I keep, which I think is mostly a good thing (it's only "mostly" because I also worry that my scrupulousness might be a sign that I'm trying to protect myself from ever losing that much again).

You should absolutely hold on to things that are dear to you and remind you of your family or important moments. But it is not good for anyone to live in the past all the time: It makes it seem as if the good times are over, and makes today feel less important than yesterday.

THROW THINGS AWAY IMMEDIATELY

After a vacation or special event, choose the things you want to keep for the memories, and immediately ditch everything else. It is much easier to get rid of things when they aren't reminders of the past, so don't let things sit around if you don't want to keep them. I try to go through my handbag once a week and chuck away all the trash that tends to settle in it like dust. It's remarkable how even something like the stub of a cinema ticket for a film you didn't much like can feel sentimental if you discover it two years later, when it reminds you of the ex you went with. At this point, the nostalgia it evokes makes chucking it out difficult.

It's much easier if you regularly weed through any areas of your home where this stuff collects, setting aside anything truly special and culling the rest.

KEEP TRYING NEW THINGS

All the evidence and our own experience show that we remember new or unusual things better than things we do day in, day out. Therefore, if you want to create strong memories, try as many new things as you can. The distinctiveness of each memory will make them more vivid in your mind, with or without attendant mementos, helping you to move more lightly.

You Might Not Need That

I f there is a physical manifestation of comfort, love, and safety, it is one's own bed. It is the emotional backstop, the place we crawl to when we are sick, or sad, or tired. Yet it is also the place where we are most vulnerable. In bed, we are asleep and defenseless, or naked and exposed; it is where some of us will give birth and most of us will die. It is the site of the deepest love and the greatest betrayals. Our beds are so personal to us that we let only a tiny handful of people sit on them, and an even smaller number get in. We get so used to the exact texture of our own bed that it can be a struggle to sleep in an unfamiliar one. At the end of a once-in-a-lifetime vacation, we tell ourselves that going home isn't all bad—after all, we'll be able to sleep in our own bed. We yearn for the comfort of our beds like a child extending their arms to a parent, wanting to be picked up.

My bed had been where I had been perfectly cozy and in total pain. I had slept in it night after night next to my ex; it was where I had lain for hours after he left, staring at the ceiling, too tired to get up.

When I moved to the new flat, a friend of a friend gave me a bed and mattress he didn't need any more. The first few nights I wriggled around in it, acquainting myself with its unknown landscape. The mattress was much softer than the one I was used to, and I sank deeply into it, feeling cosseted and comfortable in an unfamiliar way.

★ ★ ★

In the first few years after the fire, I replaced the things that I considered necessities bit by bit, as I could afford them. That included copies of my favorite books, some cushions for the sofa, and pictures to soften the walls. While nothing sentimental could ever be replaced, I wanted to create a new feeling of home.

I became obsessed with looking at what other people counted as necessities—and how, often, it was quite little. I didn't have far to look: My flatmate Claudia, who I've known since I was a teenager, is very tidy and particular about what we bring into our home. One week she went on a business trip to Switzerland. As her flight was taking off I texted her: "Enjoy! By the way, I won't be cross if you buy a cuckoo clock." She replied, "Helen, *I* would be cross if I bought a cuckoo clock."

When I enter a friend's house for the first time, I take my time looking around, trying to see how they approached their stuff. My friend John and I have roughly the same interests, and the desire to talk about them for hours on end. But the second I stepped over his doorstep for the first time, I realized the gaping chasm between us. His flat was tidy, and frighteningly so.

He gave me a tour of the small living room, which was so sparsely furnished it felt like he'd just moved in. On the mantelpiece were two matching plants, positioned so symmetrically that I wondered if he'd done it with a ruler. On the table, a chess board was laid out ready to play, like he was a character in a spy novel. The single decorative item in the entire flat was a framed black-and-white drawing on the wall. It was a portrait of John.

The only real sign of his life in the flat was the wall that was half-covered by white shelves, holding hundreds of books— mostly history and philosophy, divided by topic and then year. He said no when I asked to borrow a novel, then later scolded me for not handling a book tenderly enough. When he wasn't looking, I took one out and put it back on another shelf to see if he would notice. He did.

I was intrigued by the intense sense of strictness and order, and said so. He fought against a proud smile, then reached up on tiptoes to open a small door at the top of the shelves, which opened to reveal a pot of pens, a neat stack of notebooks, and some old bank statements in a folder. "Look at this—it's my messy cupboard!" he said. I told him that we might have different understandings of the word messy.

His sense of order was fiercely defended. When I arrived, I took my shoes off and put them to the side, by the fireplace. He picked them up and put them in a specific place by the door, the toes touching the wall at a perfect right angle. His fridge was nearly empty; his bedroom was cold and sparse. The strictness of it all made me feel slightly on edge, fretting that I was doing something wrong. I sat upright on the sofa, worried that he might see me as a mess that needed to be swept up and put outside.

★ ★ ★

As I walked home, I thought about places that felt truly comfortable. A year and a half after the fire, I went to Barcelona with two close girlfriends. One morning, the three of us walked up Carmel Hill to Parque Güell, designed by the art nouveau architect Antoni Gaudí at the beginning of the twentieth century. His major influence was the natural world, whose organic shapes he channeled into rounded windows and softly sloping ceilings. He used straight lines only when absolutely necessary.

The park is a perfect example of his principles for design. Its steps, walls, and benches move with the hills rather than fighting against them; its tortuous paths wind left and right, bringing visitors on an adventure, with surprise sculptures or porticos around each corner.

The three of us walked to the top of the hill and sat on the famous blue tiled benches that undulate like waves, looking down at the park, which flowed out before us. With each flourish and rounded edge I saw, I felt more relaxed. Nothing was being forced into a box where it didn't quite fit; everything was allowed to be, just as it was. How could a park, home to living trees and animals, look any other way?

I wanted to carry that peace with me and bring some of it into my new home. I would never be able to create complete order, and that was OK. Instead, I could try to recreate the welcoming feel of the city, allowing anyone who crossed the threshold to shrug off their worries like they were taking off a heavy coat. Being there would feel as natural as breathing. It would be home.

If I were perfect, I could have captured this feeling in my mind, or by taking a photograph. But I am not perfect, so I got a few carefully chosen souvenirs: three prints of things I had seen in the city. They were all different sizes and didn't totally work together, but I didn't mind. I hung them wonkily above my bed in gold frames.

★ ★ ★

A little while later, I scrambled to find wrapping paper. The drawer where it should have been was filled with packets of seeds I was never going to plant, old recipe cards, extra screws from flat-pack furniture that I hadn't put together correctly. Eventually, I found the tape and paper—lodged under a tire pump for a bike I no longer owned. I wrapped the present quickly, then threw the things back into the drawer, amazed that there was so much stuff in there just over a year after the fire. I didn't need it, I didn't like it, and it was adding friction to my life.

Just over a year after moving in, the bookcase held several rows of paperbacks, there was a set of decorative teacups in the kitchen, and in every drawer there were bits and bobs. Oddly,

I couldn't particularly remember buying many of these things. When I had people over they laughed, saying they would never have been able to tell that I had lost all my possessions to a fire.

Those first months rattling around my empty flat after the fire were illuminating—I saw that, to survive, I needed almost nothing. But over time, my flat had filled up again. Some of the things I liked, some had arrived by accident, and others I had convinced myself I needed. But how could that be true, if I had survived without them before? What exactly did I need—and what does it even mean to need something?

In a 1943 paper called "A Theory of Human Motivation," the American psychologist Abraham Maslow put forward a theory that summarized and categorized human needs. He said that our needs arranged themselves into hierarchies, meaning that some are more crucial than others, and that only once the most basic have been met do we start worrying about the others. In popular culture, this paper is often portrayed as a triangle called Maslow's hierarchy of needs, a version of which you have probably seen. The triangle is structured so that the most potent needs are at the bottom—physiological necessities like food, water, or air—with the needs becoming less urgent toward the top.

The idea that some needs are more needed than others can sound a little strange. If something is truly necessary for life, then surely its status as a need wouldn't be conditional? The theory says that some things are only considered needs under certain circumstances: You might not feel lonely and in need of friendship if you are life-threateningly thirsty.

This relates to the ideas of scarcity that we looked at previously, including how the mind "tunnels" to focus on the lack of fundamental things like clean water or heating. But Maslow also subtly introduces the blurred boundaries between wants and needs by describing humans as "a perpetually wanting animal," reflecting our fluid use of language on this topic. We need a home to shelter in at night. Once we have one, we need a bed to sleep in. When we have a bed, we need to buy bed sheets that match the curtains.

Our perception of what we need, and how much, isn't always correct.

Myths about What We Need

One of the reasons we are so confused is because of advertising: an industry that uses psychological research to convince us that many of our wants are in fact needs.

One common psychological technique used in advertising is called anchoring, a cognitive bias discovered by the psychologists Amos Tversky and Daniel Kahneman. In a 1974 study they asked people to spin a roulette wheel that was weighted to stop on either 10 or 65, and then to guess the percentage of African countries that were members of the United Nations.[1] The outcome of the roulette spin and geopolitics are clearly unrelated, and yet the experiment showed that our minds couldn't completely disconnect them. Participants who spun a 10 on average estimated that 25 percent of African nations were in the UN, but those who spun a 65 estimated it to be 45 percent. It was as if people couldn't quite get the first number out of their minds, and so they used it as a starting point for their estimate—the first number becoming an "anchor" around which they based their workings.

The "rules" about what we need to do or buy can often be tied up with worries about how other people see us. A viral TikTok video from 2021 showed a woman telling viewers that underwear should be thrown away every six to nine months, as apparently washing does not get it sufficiently clean. She offered no evidence to back up this claim, neither proving that cleaning isn't enough nor explaining why that particular timescale was chosen, or why the timescale is fixed and doesn't depend on how many times you've worn them. Gynecologists came out to rebut this claim, saying that underwear is not particularly dirty compared to other clothes, and the idea that it is stems from incorrect notions about the purity and cleanliness of women's bodies. But it didn't matter whether or not the claim was correct: It had already spread. The first I heard of it was a friend relaying it, as if it were gospel truth, over a drink. I'd casually asked what she'd been up to that day, and she said she'd just come from Marks & Spencer, where she'd been buying new panties. "Some of mine I'd had for two years," she said. "Can you imagine how gross that is?" I could, in fact: At that moment I was wearing a pair of underwear that I'd had for the best part of a decade.

By hearing a false rule about what she needs, my friend had started to feel ashamed of herself. She felt she was doing something deeply embarrassing and weird—as if she'd missed a crucial memo that everyone else had received. She felt a need twice over: firstly, to buy new underwear, and secondly, to assuage her embarrassment and be normal like everyone else.

The People Shaping Our Shopping

One of the early pioneers of shopping science was Paco Underhill. He founded the research company Envirosell in 1986, which has given advice on shopping behavior to companies as big as McDonald's, Sony, and Starbucks. Over the decades, Underhill and his employees have observed thousands upon thousands of shoppers, noting how they shopped, and from that worked out subtle and often unnoticeable ways to encourage them to buy more. He put many of his findings into a bestselling book called *Why We Buy.*

I found it a slightly concerning read, showing as it does how retailers can easily convince us to buy more without us realizing it. A few examples: The width of aisles is chosen precisely so that they're narrow enough for the greatest number of products to be put in front of you, but not so narrow that people brush past you from behind, which can feel claustrophobic and lead to abandoned purchases. The height at which products are displayed is important too—things that appeal to children should be low enough that they can grab them and put them into their parents' cart. The longer you spend in a shop, the more you tend to spend, which means the store is designed to encourage lingering: There could be a chair outside the changing room to keep shopping companions happy while waiting, or a "speed bump" of a low table displaying shirts or sweaters right inside the door that stops you from immediately rushing around. Shops will prominently display baskets, sometimes even employing people to stand and offer them to customers, and there's a reason why: 75 percent of people who take one will buy something, compared to 34 percent of people who don't.[2] Inside supermarkets and department stores, brands fight for the most advantageous slots. A cosmetics company in a department store will pay more for a booth that is slightly away from the entrance, allowing people to shop for makeup without feeling exposed. A food brand will pay well to be put at the end of a supermarket aisle, the endcap, which will be seen by more people as they walk through the store.

Sometimes, the influence that shop layout can have on our behavior is so strong that it feels alarming. For example, take the supermarkets that put candy and junk food on display around the checkout, a prominent location that shoppers and their children might stand in front of for some time. These displays are so effective at selling us food we don't need that they have been called a "risk factor for obesity and chronic disease" in an article in the *New England Journal of Medicine*.[3]

These checkouts were perhaps even too effective at selling, to the point where it became noticeable. Coming under pressure from parents, some supermarkets offered candy-free checkouts. But the drop in sales wasn't popular with confectioners, who fought back, writes Underhill. They instead secured slots on endcaps to the aisles that sold baby food, knowing that they would have a good chance of being seen there by children out with their parents.

(It should be noted that the UK government has wised up to both of these approaches: Unhealthy food is now banned from being displayed either at checkouts or endcaps. The digital versions have been banned too—no unhealthy food can be put in front of shoppers on homepages or checkout pages of shopping websites.)[4]

I speak to Underhill from one of his homes, an apartment in Manhattan. He says that at this point in his career, he has been successful enough that he can be choosy about his clients, and picks just "virtuous" ones like museums and natural food companies. He says he "probably" regrets some of the companies he has worked with, but at the beginning he was "doing what people do—taking the work that got offered to me." He adds that while the influence of companies on what we buy can be strong, people could arm themselves by reading another of his books, *How We Eat*, which proposes ways in which people can choose food that is better for themselves and for the planet. Whether or not this is a fair fight is debatable, I think: While all of us shopping in the modern world will be subject to these selling tricks, only a small handful will read the book.

From what I learned from his book, and from speaking to him, I think it would be wise to be extremely wary when interacting with retailers, and to see them as adversaries rather than friends. It seems sensible to question any information a shop provides, aside from that which is legally binding. In the book, Underhill quotes an executive at a clothing brand for young women explaining how they buy cheaply made T-shirts in Sri Lanka, then sew in washing instructions in French and English.

While never directly stating that the clothes are made in France, the conditions are created in which that assumption could be made—with the customer therefore believing the item to be a premium product that warrants a higher price. In another example (one that really shows its age), Underhill writes how he told Blockbuster stores to put old videos on their recently returned carts, encouraging people to rent them by giving the impression that they were popular.

But there could be a more freeing way to think about these tricks. If corporations are putting so much effort into trying to get us to buy chocolate or T-shirts or whatever, then do we really need it in the first place?

When Minimalism Helps, and When It Hinders

Life was good for Colin Wright. In 2009 he was twenty-four, running a branding business in Los Angeles and making more money than he had ever thought possible. He had a lovely girlfriend, an impressive apartment, and a closet full of expensive clothes.

But there was one problem. Wright looked ahead along his career path and saw his bosses, who were deeply unhappy. Sure, they made a lot of money, but they worked grueling hours and many had been divorced multiple times. Wright wanted none of it.

After a revelatory weekend away to the Grand Canyon, Wright came back and decided he wanted to make a change.

He gave himself a deadline of four months to quit his job and leave the country to go travelling.

Before doing so, he would need to sort out his things. Over that four-month period he got rid of everything—donating it or just throwing it away—until he could fit all he had into a backpack.

His new life of travel allowed him a level of freedom he didn't have before. Instead of working himself to the bone in the corporate world he forged a meaningful career as an author and blogger on his website, Exile Lifestyle.

Since leaving LA, Wright has been to sixty-five countries. He has brought home precisely zero souvenirs.

★ ★ ★

Minimalism might sometimes seem stoic or ascetic; a philosophy of forgoing earthly pleasures for a greater purpose. But there is nothing chilly or joyless about what Wright describes. In our conversation, he never talks about denying himself delights, but instead about sharing them out.

In his former life in LA, he owned eight(!) computers at the same time. At first, clearing them and his other stuff out felt like "pulling teeth," he said, until his mindset changed to one of generosity with others: "If I get rid of this extra computer I'm not using, someone else gets to use this really great thing that can be a tool for them."

While minimalism helped Wright to free himself of a life he didn't want and discover one that he did, there have been a few times when it has made his life harder. I speak to him from his rented apartment in Milwaukee, Wisconsin, where he has lived for two years now—the longest he has stayed anywhere since he packed up his home in LA.

After living out of a backpack for over a decade, building a home has not always been easy. It was difficult to get out of the habit of viewing every new purchase through the lens of: "Can I pack this up into a travel bag and leave tomorrow?" he said.

It took several months to get used to the "weird concept" of buying a sofa. He couldn't pack it up into a bag, and how could he say he needed one if he already had something to sit on—a desk chair?

But over time, the idea became less "weird." If he sat on his desk chair in the evenings, there was nowhere for his girlfriend to sit, and having friends over was out of the question. Unlike when he was travelling, his apartment wasn't "just a location that you're squatting [in]," it was the place where he invited friends to, where his girlfriend could lay out her paints and work on her art, where the two of them could spend quiet evenings together. It had become a home.

And with that shift, the strict minimalism he'd followed no longer fit.

No-Buy Month

Realizing that I had been wrong before about what I needed— and that there are so many different interpretations of what we do actually need—I decided to conduct some experiments.

I came across no-buy challenges a few years ago on YouTube. In lockdown, I naturally found myself buying a lot less—of course, I wasn't spending anything on going out, but I also massively reduced the number of physical things I bought. Without my daily commute, which usually brought me past several shops, there was far less temptation than before. There was also a subtle shift in my mind caused by the fact that I wasn't going anywhere. I had what I needed, and my idea of what I needed wasn't constantly being challenged by seeing what other people had, since I wasn't seeing any other people, let alone what they had. I even felt a sense of imperviousness to the ads being served up on social media; the shining models felt so distant from my life, which I spent wearing tracksuits and joining the fad for bread making, that they were almost irrelevant.

A few months in, I started seeing videos made by people who had given up buying anything other than strict necessities for a month, a year, or sometimes longer. The idea was intriguing, given what I had already learned from a few months of buying very little. I watched more and more. The way these people had worked out what was needed and cut out everything else reminded me of how the lockdowns had pared my life right down to its basics.

For some people, it was a straight financial decision, undertaken to save for a wedding or to help toward a deposit for a home. Other people went on these journeys not to save money but for something closer to spiritual reasons, where they hoped that by refraining from the hedonistic pleasures of shopping they could focus on a higher set of values. But it should be noted that these challenges are voluntary; being in a position where strict necessities are all you can afford is much, much harder, and very different from cutting back out of choice.

I decided that there was no better way to see how this would work out than to try it for myself. It felt wild to jump into not buying anything for a full year, so I settled on a month. At the end of one October, I decided I would try it for the whole of November.

Of course, like anything, the devil is in the details. If your no-buy challenge lasts more than a few days, then inevitably it becomes something more like a low-buy or buy-only-essentials challenge. There will eventually be something that you need: your train ticket to work, or shampoo, or food. Saying to yourself that you'll only buy what you need won't work. That is pretty much how we live already, with so many purchases justified along the lines of a false "need"—you had a bad day so you need to get a pick-me-up on the way home, or you are going to a wedding so you need to buy a new suit.

It's therefore generally recommended that you set out a robust set of principles before beginning, and that they are clear and comprehensive enough that no decisions need to be made on the hoof. This refers to a psychological principle called the hot-cold empathy gap: the difference between the decisions you might make in a logical frame of mind and those that you make in the heat of the moment. For example, when going to a party, you might commit before getting there to having just one drink in order to be able to drive home. If you decide how many to have when you're already one down at the party, your decision might be quite different.

When approaching a no-buy challenge, people generally advise doing the same and deciding what you are and aren't allowed to spend money on before it begins. You will probably make a more rational decision if you decide a week before it starts that you do not need more beauty products than you would if you encounter perfume on sale a few days into the month.

So I opened a new note on my phone and made a list of what was allowed and what wasn't. Allowed: replacements for food, medicine, and essential toiletries (soap OK, nail varnish not); a Travelcard to get to work; a small sum for drinks with friends; and pre-existing subscriptions for things like the gym. Not allowed: clothes, books, nonessential home items like candles, and starting new subscriptions. As far as these lists go, this one is pretty slack—others would rule out spending on nonphysical things like gym memberships or a budget for seeing friends. I felt that this went too far for me; exercising seemed like an essential purchase, and I was single, so seeing my friends in the evenings was incredibly important. Also, I felt that the goal was to reassess my relationship with buying *stuff*, not with spending money in general.

★ ★ ★

The last few days of October had a strange feeling to them, like I was preparing for a great expedition. It reminded me of a TV show I'd seen about a group of Victorian explorers who had packed up several years' worth of provisions to get them through a voyage to the Arctic, except that had involved hundreds of men preparing for an exceptionally tough few years in the wilderness, whereas I was going to be spending a month mostly in my flat in a big city. I told myself that I was being ridiculous and that there was no reason to prepare. After all, I would be allowed to buy anything that I truly needed.

I'd watched others online fall into a particular trap before starting one of these challenges: readying themselves to buy nothing by buying a whole set of new things first. If people were challenging themselves to not eat out during their no-buy, then some of them started by buying a pretty new set of matching lunch containers for their homemade food. Others planned to not buy any personal care products for the month by stocking up on their supplies. It felt like the same mental trap that I had seen time and again in my journey to re-evaluate my relationship with materialism: We tell ourselves that everything will be OK just as soon as we've bought the next thing. I saw a similar urge within online minimalist spaces, with some people putting off decluttering until they had got just the right storage boxes/shoe racks/coat hangers. It seemed to be just another way of telling ourselves that contentment is somewhere else, rather than something that comes from within.

I wanted to stay away from those lines of thinking, and so committed to not buying anything special or stocking up beforehand. If I truly needed it, I would be able to get it.

Although my rules did allow me to buy food, I felt that I should stick to the spirit of the law and purchase just what I really needed. That meant that I needed to take stock of what

I already had in the cupboards and freezer. OK, there was nothing particularly exciting in there, but certainly enough to keep me fed for about a week. There was a bag of oats that I could use to make porridge instead of buying bread to make toast in the mornings, and in the freezer there were a few bags of mixed vegetables and a box of veggie sausages that would be fine for dinner. In a global and historical context, I was lucky to have so much in my cupboards, even if I had been trained to think that my every craving should be catered to.

I also thought about the food I was eating outside of home, which was substantial. Ever since I can remember, I have eaten about twice as much as the average woman, which means that my pockets are usually lined with wrappers from cereal bars and cheese strings. I also tend to be a little chaotic, so I often end up not having enough time to eat breakfast or lunch, and have to scramble together meals from the vending machine at work. This system clearly wasn't working, so I hoped that taking more time to think about how I was shopping for food might help.

In hindsight, November was one of the worst months I could have chosen for the no-buy challenge. After a warm and golden October, it was an unusually cold November, where the days alternated between sleet and rain. It was already miserable enough without cutting down on treats.

I had also just started a new job, and my desire to make a good first impression drove me to work like Hermione Granger and cancel almost all of my social plans. For a month, I lived like a shadow, scuttling home every night and getting to bed early so I could wake up before dawn to get to the office in good time.

The only daylight I got was fifteen minutes at lunchtime, when I forced myself out to walk around the block.

The first week was strange, so empty that it felt almost like a spiritual exercise. I wrote fifty pages in my diary in just seven days. Some passages were short lists of things I hadn't bought; others were long solipsistic passages about why I found it so hard to just sit still and do nothing for a bit.

After a fortnight, I snapped, unable to cope with the boredom. I am an incorrigible extrovert, and spending so much time at home on my own after working silently in the day was driving me crazy. One Thursday night I left work feeling like my body was a bag of snakes—I had so much pent-up stress and energy that I was practically wriggling. I texted a friend saying that I needed a drink and hopefully even a dance, and soon.

He suggested we meet near my house, at a pub that had live music. There was some obscure Dutch band playing that I hadn't heard of, but it didn't matter. Five drinks and two hours of dancing in, my hair stuck to my scalp with sweat, I was feeling a lot looser. I wandered over to the merchandise stall, which was manned by a young guy who was a distant relation of one of the members of the band. Some new mood came over me in an instant, like the clicking of a camera, and I decided that I wanted to buy something. I pulled out my credit card (big mistake to have even brought it out with me) and bought a scarf, a T-shirt, and a vinyl record. I do not own a record player.

★ ★ ★

Aside from this slip-up, by the end of the month, I was beginning to see the appeal of the challenge. There was the most obvious—I had saved money, about £200 ($260), which would otherwise have gone to random bits and bobs. This number would have been even higher if I hadn't had that daft night at the pub.

I had some vague idea of how I had saved this money. There were the casual nights in the pub that I hadn't had during the first two weeks of monastic purity. I had also stopped myself from buying something to wear for a party and saved myself at least one trip to the supermarket by double-checking the spice rack and finding what I needed. But the rest was a bit of a mystery—by telling myself that little splurges were out of bounds, it was like I had stopped seeing opportunities to spend. The mental shift this caused was subtle, yet revolutionary.

Toward the end of the month I started to become aware of a much greater sense of calm in my mind. It took me a few days to understand why that might be, until a trip to a big department store. Before my no-buy month, I typically would have taken a cart and started by first wandering through the clothes and home-wares, looking at every single thing they stocked to see whether there was anything that I liked/wanted/needed/was good value.

This would take a long time. By the time I had deemed my browsing complete, it might be forty-five minutes since I'd come into the store. Lots of times I would come out pushing an empty cart—meaning forty-five minutes had in essence been completely wasted. Other times I might get something small like a notebook, which I had let myself buy to make it easier to say no to the expensive thing that I actually wanted.

Not only does setting a no-buy rule save all that time, but in my case it also saved me from the accompanying mental conflict. If you know when you walk into a supermarket that you're only buying the food you need, you don't need to worry about whether or not you're missing out on a good deal on baking pans. There is peace in being able to tell yourself that if you needed to buy a frying pan, you would be able to, under the rules. But if you do not need one, then you do not need to waste time or effort thinking about it. Done.

I came out of the store feeling much more peaceful than I normally would. Why was that? There was the time saved and the reduced decision-making, of course, but something else too: When I wasn't constantly thinking about the possibility of buying new stuff, I wasn't thinking of what I already had as "not good enough." Instead of seeing my life as something that needed material improvement, I saw it as whole and complete—with the understanding that if that changed, any true need would be looked after.

There was another sensation. When I had quieted the part of my mind that was constantly scanning for things to buy, it was as if my viewpoint of the world changed. No longer was I seeing myself from the outside and fretting about how others saw me. It was like my eyes were put back in my head, and I could look outward at the world, instead of inward at myself. When I stopped trying to address the little worries I felt, they stopped bothering me. I saw them for what they were—irrelevant.

For this challenge to have a genuine impact, there needs to be a path out of it afterward, one that helps you to bring the lessons of your no-buy month into your everyday life. Having rules, even loose ones, are effective because they take the effort out of making decisions. If you're a vegetarian, you don't quibble when you're offered a chicken sandwich, you just say no.

I set myself a rough set of rules. From now on, shopping would be either "on" or "off"—most of the time I know I don't need or truly want anything, so it's switched off, with no browsing and no worrying about what I'm missing out on. When I do need or really want something, I list what it is and wait, to test if that feeling stays. If so, I will open a shopping season briefly and allow myself to browse. When I'm satisfied, it's off again.

Experimenting with buying nothing other than necessities was freeing and uplifting. It's easy to slip back into bad habits, so I'm planning on doing a full no-buy month every year in order to reset my sense of need.

★ ★ ★

True needs do not go away if we ignore them. No matter how much we try to push them down, they will always bob up like a buoy, reminding us that we are hungry or thirsty or cold. The itchy feeling of need is giving us helpful information, pointing us to things that will make us feel better.

The sort of "need" that falls away in a few hours, or when you've been distracted by another "need," is the complete opposite. It not only tells us nothing helpful, but it can be actively harmful. It leads us to waste money, of course, but also encourages something worse—a feeling of constant dissatisfaction. It tells us that our lives are lacking, that we will only be happy when we have reached the magical time in the future when all our needs are satisfied. Fake needs create unhappiness out of thin air.

My no-buy experiment was so freeing and uplifting that it seemed to permanently flip a switch in my mind. I have absolutely bought some things I don't need now that the challenge is over, but I've seen them as just that—fun things that add to my life rather than necessities. Instead of seeing shopping as a process of lacking something, buying it, then returning to a neutral baseline, I now see that I am already at the baseline, and shopping is a short boost above that baseline. It is a chance to enjoy occasional pleasure rather than a solution to a problem. There never was a problem.

FINAL THOUGHTS

CHALLENGE YOURSELF WHEN YOU THINK "I NEED THIS"

Our first feeling about what we "need" is often misguided. Earlier we talked about how needs tend to be specific. If your fridge breaks down, you need to get it fixed: It has a very particular function and your need for it won't go away by buying something else. You don't need a new coat for winter if the one you bought last year fits perfectly.

When you feel compelled to buy something out of necessity, question that feeling. What else could take its place? What will happen if you don't buy it? Will you still notice its absence in a week, a month, or a year?

There are plenty of things that you should buy if they will improve your life, but don't let yourself falsely justify things by saying they're essential. Not only does this lead you to buying things that you don't need, but it also creates a false feeling of obligation that will take away a lot of the joy from the item. If you see something as simply filling a hole in your life, buying it will seem like a chore rather than a treat.

SHOP SMART

Now that some of the tricks of retailers have been revealed, you can be wise to them. If you're just browsing or want one or two things, don't pick up a basket. Look left and right, high and low, to see all the options: Don't just settle for what's directly ahead. And be very skeptical about the information you're given.

BE RUTHLESS

Your home is not a place of last resort for dumping things. If there are things that you don't want or need, donate them or throw them away. Worrying about waste is a good thing, but keeping a set of fancy glasses that you don't like and never use means that *they are already being wasted*. It would be much more efficient to donate them and allow someone else to get use from them. The fact that you were given them as a present is not a good enough reason to keep them around. The error was in giving someone a bulky gift without checking if they might like it, not in you getting rid of them. You haven't failed by not using them.

Treat your home as a place for you to live in, not a storage container for things that can't go anywhere else. After you've donated the unwanted items, you can learn the lesson of not picking up similar stuff in the future.

MAKE RULES ABOUT WHAT TO KEEP

You can create a set of guidelines that delineate what you need to keep around. Mine differ slightly depending on what the item is, but here are some examples.

Books: If I read a book and didn't enjoy it, I get rid of it. I do not consider whether displaying it on my shelf will make me look impressive or smart. My home is a place to keep the things that make me happy and reflect my character. It's not about creating a false character to advertise to others.

Clothes: When spring-cleaning, I ask whether I have worn something in the past year. If I haven't, I put it on immediately and wear it that day (weather dependent). Usually, there's a reason why I haven't worn it—maybe the sleeves are a bit uncomfortable, or the label is itchy. If I feel a slight sinking feeling about wearing it that day, I almost always get rid of it. If wearing it is annoying, then I will never pick it out of my wardrobe and put it on in the morning. It doesn't matter what it looks like or where it came from—it is taking up space that I don't have to spare.

Electronics: To avoid the usual buildup, I get rid of any charger or cord that I don't recognize. Almost every time, I don't recognize it because I haven't used it for years and no longer need it.

Beauty Is Necessary

I was given a pair of patterned champagne flutes for my birthday one year by two friends. We were broke students in the middle of our degrees, living in small flats that usually had at least one significant structural problem. The flutes therefore stood out: The glass they were made from was etched with delicate swirls and loops, and was so thin that I felt nervous every time I clinked them together. Of course, I loved them because of the happy friendships they represented, but there was something else too: They were so pretty that it made me happy just to look at them on the shelf. And on the shelf they spent most of their time, because I was afraid of breaking them.

There was something particularly beautiful about the fact that there were just two of them. Flutes are for celebrating, but a pair can only be used for the most special moments of all—something so wonderful has happened that it justifies opening a bottle between two, which must be toasted immediately, before there's time to tell the rest of the world. They'd been through an intimate New Year's Eve for two, a birthday where we'd stayed up till midnight to toast it in, graduations, and new jobs. Moments that deserved beauty.

A number of years ago, I went on holiday to Italy with my friend Immy. We drove around Tuscany, going from lunch to dinner. After a few days of drinking and sunbathing, we decided we should probably get up and do something, and so we went to Florence.

We wandered around the Uffizi Gallery, which was too much for our woolly heads to take in. By the time we got to the Botticelli rooms, my feet were aching, and so I tucked myself to the side, trying to get out of the crowds for a minute and find a wall to rest against. I moved to the side of the *Birth of Venus* and looked out into the room, scanning for Immy so I could do our secret signal for "Diet Coke needed soon." I couldn't see her, but I spotted a man who was gazing at the painting just to my side. He was standing completely upright, as if the teacher had just walked in the room, but with his head tipped upward, toward the heavens. And he was sobbing: thick tears sliding down his face, his chest bobbing up and down as he tried to stay quiet.

The sight of him crying set tears pricking in my own eyes. Whatever he was seeing in the painting was personal to him and a mystery to anyone else. But I could have a reasonable guess at what he was feeling: awe, in the face of beauty.

Definitions of Beauty

People have tried for thousands of years to come up with a formal definition of beauty. Some say that it has to do with how something looks or sounds, while others believe it can also apply to intangible things like ideas or concepts. There is an argument that beauty is valuable because it is inherently useless, offering a purer experience because it doesn't offer you any material benefit. Some describe beauty as a positive force that can inspire us to pursue noble ideals—or a chase that becomes destructive. Beauty can feel welcoming and warm, or can overwhelm and feel more like awe or dread.

The multifaceted nature of beauty isn't just a philosophical problem. Some of the difficulties of defining beauty come out in a 2010 report by polling company Ipsos Mori.[1] To try to work out what ordinary people thought about beauty in their surroundings, pollsters interviewed a group of people in Sheffield, in northern England. They found the group to be hesitant when asked to say what beauty meant to them, with many of them reportedly left speechless by the question. Others gave wondrous responses, some describing the experience of finding something beautiful as "sacred or privately meaningful," while others said that part of what made beauty so important was its indefinable quality.

That same point is made by people throughout the report—being around beautiful things feels good, and in a way that is different to other pleasures in life. Or as one respondent put it, "When you're surrounded by beautiful buildings, or something that looks extraordinary, straight away you're more up about things."

Throughout this chapter we will look at beauty from different points of view: from philosophers who use reasoning to make sense of it; psychologists who have measured its effect on the brain; and ordinary people who know beauty by how it feels. I think it is something else, too: a fundamental human need, without which we can fall into despair. And often, we are using our stuff to fulfill that need.

In The Eye(s) of the Beholder(s)

There is nothing quite like a book club for turning people you thought were your best friends into complete strangers. Just when you think you know someone, they turn around and say that the dullest novel you've ever read was "luminous."

Even though I know logically that opinions differ, that doesn't lessen the shock I feel when someone sees beauty where I don't, and vice versa. Everyone has had some version of this conversation, whether it was on the way out of the cinema with a friend or arguing with your partner about which rug would look nice in the living room. We say beauty is in the eye of the beholder, but when beauty strikes us, it does so with such force that we simply cannot believe there is anyone who can't see it.

One of the major disagreements in aesthetics—the branch of philosophy that considers beauty—is whether beauty is subjective or objective. Is beauty a verifiable quality that is inherent in an object, or is it an entirely subjective response that exists only in the mind of the person observing it?

If we search the real world for answers, it seems that it lies somewhere in the middle.

Yes, a painting that is beautiful to one person might be hideous to another, but there is some agreement when it comes to what is and isn't beautiful. Most people find smiling babies and ocean sunsets beautiful. And generally, they do not feel the same about concrete and gloomy days. We could say that certain attributes correlate with people reporting they find an object beautiful, but they don't guarantee it.

The Science of Beauty

It is not only philosophers and artists who study the meaning and purpose of beauty: It is also a subject of study for scientists, who try to work out what our brains are doing when we perceive something as "beautiful." While beauty in some fields might be praised for, or even defined by, its uselessness, much of the scientific research around it challenges this assumption and tries to work out why humans have evolved to feel beauty.

Professor Anjan Chatterjee of the Perelman School of Medicine at the University of Pennsylvania is one of the key scientists in this area, and runs his own lab that investigates the effects of beauty in the brain. It can be a controversial area of study, he says, with some philosophers believing that a scientific approach to beauty is a "categorical mistake" that fails to capture "the profound nature of beauty."

Through his lab and the work of others, we have come to learn that there is no one area of the brain responsible for processing "beauty"; the phenomenon is a mixture of many things. While the brain has clearly defined areas that process information about things like language or movement, beauty sets off a complex reaction at various locations across the brain.

Beauty causes pleasure. The typical evolutionary case for pleasure is straightforward: It guides us toward things that will help us survive and reproduce, like food, warmth, or sex. Following this line of reasoning would explain why we find other people beautiful, as it draws us together to bond and have children.

But in other cases it doesn't work, especially if we follow the definition of beauty as a useless pleasure. Immanuel Kant, the Enlightenment philosopher, distinguishes beauty from other pleasures by calling it a "disinterested interest," that is, liking without wanting.[2] While the pleasure of looking at a beautiful face might compel us to move closer to the person, we can get pleasure from a painting without it making us want to do anything.

Liking and wanting usually go together, says Chatterjee, and in fact form some of the most fundamental behaviors known in living things. Liking is typically a sign that something will help us survive and reproduce, and it leads to an "approach" response of wanting something, the dopamine-led activity that we discussed earlier. This is common to many forms of life: Even single-cell amoebas move toward things that will aid their survival, and away from things that are toxic.

There are two ways to think about why our minds can sense this "disinterested interest," or liking without wanting, in scientific terms. It could be a by-product of other evolved behaviors—perhaps the softly flowing contours of a beautiful vase remind us of the shape of a human body. Or perhaps beauty is critical in some way that is not immediately obvious. I think it could be the latter.

Beauty in Nature

If you scroll through the photos on my phone, you will notice a pattern. They tend to cluster around three themes: people I love, delicious food I've eaten, and landscapes I never want to forget. The first two fit neatly into the idea that pleasure is followed by the urge to action—I want to be near those people and eat that food. But how can I want a landscape? I can't own a mountain, buy a squirrel, or stroke a sunset. And yet, I find looking at them pleasurable.

Even if we can't benefit from a view of nature in the way we could a partner or a plate of pasta, our experience of beauty in the outdoors might still have been helpful for our survival as a species. One of the most straightforward examples is the near-universal love that people have for flowers. Chatterjee writes that this is hardly a mystery: flowers are "a landscape fitness indicator," which would have indicated to our ancestors areas that would be good for foraging fruit in a few weeks or months.

Similarly, he points to studies that demonstrate consistencies in the types of landscapes that we find attractive. We tend to like scenes that have "water, large trees, a focal point, changes in elevation, relatively open spaces, distant views of the horizon, and some complexity." This seems to make sense in survival terms: water to drink, trees to climb up and hide under, and a chance to see what is coming from far in the distance. On top of that, we seem to want a fine balance of "complexity" or novelty, and "coherence" or uniformity. Complexity means that a landscape has a greater chance of offering several things that we need, while regularity means that there aren't too many unpredictable features that could hinder how quickly we can process the visual information in a scene, allowing danger to strike. Some studies described something called "the savanna hypothesis," where people tend to find pictures of these wide, open grassy plains particularly beautiful, even if they have never seen one in real life.[3]

Our appreciation of natural beauty extends further than just landscapes and carries into our homes and the objects we buy. According to a study by Acumen Research and Consulting, the flowers and houseplants industry is worth $16.2 billion.[4] By and large, these plants are totally useless except for their beauty—they provide us with neither food nor shelter, merely sitting on our shelves and enjoying the sunlight. And yet this burst of beauty can do wondrous things for us. Indoor plants can lower our stress levels[5] and improve our well-being.[6]

I realize that I have used this principle in a small way in my life for some time: I always set the backgrounds of my email accounts to be photographs of forests. If I am going to be staring at the same page for several hours a day, it makes me feel slightly better to look at something green while I do it, even if it's just a photograph.

Beauty and Awe

Whether or not we believe in God, beauty can move us to feel something beyond the ordinary. I don't know whether the man I saw in the Uffizi was religious, but clearly he was experiencing something out of the ordinary, probably something approaching awe. This feeling, that we are in the presence of something extraordinary, and bigger than ourselves, provokes a sense of mystical wonder.

Writers and philosophers have long been interested in how we react to beauty in this way. Starting from the eighteenth century, the poets and artists of the Romantic movement were inspired by the idea of the "sublime"—a reaction to beauty that was so overpowering that it elicited sensations akin to fear. Often, they linked this feeling with the greatest of natural beauties, like the sheer face of a mountain range. Such scenes may feel too big for our minds to take in, showing us in comparison how small we are, which can feel exposing and frightening.

The Romantics might have thought that the sense of awe in the face of beauty was a sign of the transcendent nature of beauty or of human beings. To other people, though, such perfect beauty doesn't belong on earth; it is the manifestation of something beyond this world, and proof of divine existence.

Appreciating beauty can improve your life, reducing anxiety and depression[7] and improving your well-being.[8] Reveling in the beauty of nature can even lower your inflammation levels, a marker that can indicate your risk of serious conditions like heart disease or type 2 diabetes. Why might this be the case? It looks like it could be the feelings of awe that we experience when we notice the beauty of an object or a scene.

In *Character Strengths and Virtues: A Handbook and Classification*, psychologists Christopher Peterson and Martin Seligman classify an appreciation of beauty and excellence within a set of traits called "strengths of transcendence," along with gratitude, hope, humor, and spirituality. Their explanation is as follows: "The common theme running through these strengths of transcendence is that each allows individuals to forge connections to the larger universe and thereby provide meaning to their lives."[9]

According to the authors' classification, beauty links people together by appealing to something greater beyond our individual lives. This helps us to look up from the quotidian and to consider instead "transcendent (nonmaterial) aspects of life—whether they be called universal, ideal, sacred, or divine." You do not need to have a sophisticated understanding of the high arts for the effect to take hold: It's about the "emotional experience of awe or wonder when in the presence of beauty or excellence," which could be about fine wine or a perfect chocolate milkshake. (On reading this, my mind turned to a scene in *The Menu*, the horror/comedy film where Ralph Fiennes's chef is obsessed with perfection through haute cuisine, only finally experiencing the true ideal of food when making a cheeseburger.)

Feeling awe in the face of beauty is also related to some of the other virtues of "transcendence," such as hope. In a small but very sweet study, two psychologists in Idaho ran an experiment using their respective classes. One class was given homework whereby every week they had to note down something natural, something man-made, and an act of kindness that they found beautiful.[10] Each week, the logs were briefly discussed in class. The other class was the control and was set no work. At the end of the term, the class that was asked to keep the logs was more hopeful. This experiment makes me think of the gratitude journals that we are often encouraged to keep, and shows the benefits of taking time to see the beauty and goodness of the world.

It seems to me that experiencing awe with beauty has one main effect: It is humbling. When we contemplate Botticelli's enormous canvases and heavenly figures, we realize our imperfection. Climbing up the fells of the Lake District and looking into an ancient open valley makes us feel insignificant: We are small beings alive only for a brief moment. While this sudden curtailment of ego might feel terrifying, it can cause feelings of ecstasy at the same time. We can finally get out of our own heads, realizing that so many of the things we get caught up in are unimportant.

An overwhelming sense of beauty can also be a necessary break from the mundane elements of our daily lives. Sometimes I think about what it must have been like to attend church in medieval times. All week people must have toiled at tough labor, eating plain food, wearing brown clothes, shivering in cold houses, and spending the evenings in the near darkness with almost nothing fun to do. But on Sundays there was the chance to go somewhere completely different. For a few hours, you could experience beauty, gazing at the painted walls and listening to music. It must have felt like nothing short of magic, proof that life is more than just daily toiling, that there is something beyond that's worth striving for.

Living in Beauty

It is instantly obvious that Samuel Hughes believes in the importance of beauty. We meet in a London pub, where I find him sitting upright on a stool. He is perfectly turned out: wearing a brown tweed jacket and wine-colored silk tie, which are offset by a white pocket square and a watch with Roman numerals and a leather strap. His hair is neatly combed, and even his mannerisms are precise and seem to be chosen for aesthetic perfection: His hands gracefully sketch out shapes as he speaks, and when he needs to pull out his phone to show me a photo to illustrate a point he's making, he apologizes for the interruption.

After studying aesthetics as an undergraduate in philosophy at the University of Cambridge, Hughes has built a career around advocating for the importance of beauty. He was a researcher on the "Building Better, Building Beautiful" commission that advised the UK government on how to improve the look of new-build homes. Now he advocates for the building of more and better homes that are pleasant to the eye and create stronger communities.

As we saw above, what ordinary people find beautiful can differ greatly from what specialists prefer. In experiments, people on average like complex yet symmetrical patterns, while those with a high level of art education tend to find asymmetry and simplicity more beautiful. A similar divergence in taste has emerged in architecture, argues Hughes: While the tastes of the general public have remained remarkably static over time, the view of elite architects has gone through trend cycles.

Although architects love to design new and outrageous styles, ordinary people usually prefer to live somewhere that they find pleasing and beautiful. Although Victorian architects might have gone hell-for-leather for neo-Gothic designs, ordinary people kept and maintained their Georgian neoclassical homes. Today we find beautiful old buildings similarly compelling and prefer them to the latest trends: Despite most people thinking that new-build homes are for richer buyers, half of those who took part in a survey in 2019 thought they were ugly.[11] Buildings that are old but timelessly beautiful typically have a premium on them, and rich people "very, very rarely buy" new builds, says Hughes.

Beautiful buildings can have an amazing longevity, with people inspired to look after them well to make sure they can be enjoyed by the next generation. Even the pub we meet in is a good example. It's part of London's St Pancras station, designed by William Henry Barlow and first opened in 1868. It is a wonderful example of High Victorian style, mixing intricate decoration with engineering feats like its huge glass ceiling. After we finish our drinks, Hughes takes me on a walk around the station and points out little flourishes of the building that I would otherwise have missed. Near the entrance, every pillar has a unique capital (the blocky bit at the top), apparently the result of craftsmen allowed to experiment with nature-inspired designs. Some have leaves that twist like vines, while others are large and lush. We poke our heads into the St. Pancras Renaissance, the attached hotel designed by Sir Gilbert Scott that first opened in 1873, then shut down for a number of decades before its renovation and reopening in 2011. I love it, but I can see how it might be a little bit much for some people: a cross between a Gothic cathedral and the Gryffindor common room. No space is left undecorated, with walls covered with Christmassy red and gold wallpaper punctuated by stone faux-medieval windows. The building seems to resist the strictures of engineering, with one critic describing it as "a thing of movement, a web of stairs and endless corridors."[12] It is easy to see how the building fell out of favor with minimalists in the twentieth century.

Beyond the station is a development of shops and restaurants based around Victorian "coal drop" sheds, where coal brought by train from the north of England would be stored. These old coal sheds now house brunch spots and wine bars. In the same complex, an old grain store has been converted into an art college, and gas storage cylinders have become luxury flats. These buildings were never designed for these purposes, but their beauty meant that they were worth saving and converting into something else. They use symmetry, are familiar and yet distinct, and pay attention to detail. Because they were beautiful, they lasted.

★ ★ ★

Beautiful things are important. Perhaps their purpose isn't as immediately obvious as that of the things we looked at in the last chapter that address our physical needs for warmth and food, but they are still necessary to us. Beautiful things inspire us, encourage us through hard times, and make us turn our eyes from petty distractions toward life's greater purpose. Encountering things we find truly beautiful satisfies the needs of our minds and souls.

If you're not convinced by that argument, then I hope you can at least accept that beautiful things have material benefits. If we have things we find beautiful, we will take better care of them, cutting down on our use of resources and saving money. Many of them will outlive even us, becoming heirlooms that will be treasured by future generations. Their indefinably special quality enchants us, encouraging us to be our best selves in return.

FINAL THOUGHTS

HAVE AT LEAST ONE THING THAT YOU FIND BEAUTIFUL IN EVERY ROOM OF YOUR HOME

There is no reason why beauty should be costly. You could have a few conkers, a bunch of supermarket daffodils, a patterned teapot from a thrift shop. I have two potted plants in the loo of my flat, grown from donated cuttings. You could also show your appreciation for beauty by taking good care of everyday things. Tidy up the linen cupboard or polish your shoes. Put the shower curtain in the washing machine.

By no means is this an instruction to fill your house up with every lovely object you encounter. I do not think that would be beautiful. It is about careful, precise selection of things that you find beautiful. And treat this like it is something very important, because it is. It is a reminder to yourself that there are good things in the world, that your life has meaning and purpose, that there are ideals worth reaching for.

FOCUS ON BEAUTY

There is an art history professor at Harvard who assigns her students the following homework, in the belief that some details and interpretations can only be understood after a long period of time: Go to a gallery and spend three hours looking at just one thing.[13] She stresses that the context of this exercise—the gallery or museum—is crucial, as it takes the student away from their normal life and distractions.

Clearly this exercise can only really be recommended to students, given that almost no one else will be lucky enough to have three hours to spare for it. But I do still think there is something useful in it for all of us. When we find something beautiful, we will get so much more from it if we give it some real attention. This is part of the reason that I love the cinema: Films are much more enjoyable when your phone is switched off and no one is talking over the best bits. There's also something to be said for enjoying one thing at a time. How often do you put headphones in and listen to tinny music while you're walking along the street, missing how the golden autumn light pours on the ground like syrup?

REDUCE VISUAL NOISE

Walk around your home slowly and take note of the way different spaces make you feel. Which parts of it feel the most calming to you, and which, if any, do the opposite? If it's the latter, think about whether that might be because of the level of visual noise in an area. Arrange books on a shelf by color or size; reduce the number of trinkets on the mantelpiece. Beautiful things need space to breathe.

RELISH SMALL BEAUTIES

Buy a postcard of a painting or view that you just adore and stick it on your fridge. These examples of everyday beauty can be the most important of all—they prove that moments of wonder can be found everywhere. Appreciating beauty is not just for a lucky few: It is a fundamental part of being human.

FIND WONDER

As well as the everyday beauties, the big ones are important too. As we've seen, the overwhelming nature of some beautiful things can have a profound effect on us. Looking at a masterpiece or a great mountain range can put our petty daily problems into perspective and help us to bond with one another. Using beauty to connect with a greater power—whether through the wonder of nature, the inspiration of art, or something religious—can be one of the most meaningful experiences of our lives.

APPRECIATE NATURAL BEAUTY

Nature is one of the most common means by which we experience beauty, and lots of evidence suggests evolutionary reasons for this. The British mental health charity Mind has collected anecdotes from people explaining the significance of nature in their lives. Some are very moving. "It is hard to explain the power of nature in relieving both my physical and mental stress," reads one. "There is little more relaxing than sitting with a cup of tea looking at a hill through a window and hearing the nearby stream trickle away."[14]

For those of us not lucky enough to have a hill and a trickling stream on the other side of our windows, there are other ways to connect with nature. Small, beautiful things matter. A study found that just a single houseplant changed the lives of elderly residents of care homes.[15]

True Pleasure Lasts

Today, a Saturday in the middle of February, has been the perfect day. The air has just started to smell fresh and the sun is getting stronger, making the sky a brighter blue. I woke up early, put on old sneakers that I don't mind getting muddy, and went for a walk in the park. On the way home, I stopped to take a picture of a garden that had been overrun by sweet purple crocuses. I was nicely tired when I got home, and laid down on the sofa to look at the sun coming through the window. I had been working nonstop the whole week, which meant that today there was nothing at all for me to do. I could lie on the sofa, drink tea, and read my book. Which is what I did. It was the happiest I could be. I had time to spare.

Simple pleasures are not always so simple. Wandering round the park then sitting on your sofa might seem like one of the easiest paths to happiness that there is, but lately I hadn't found it so: I had been working so much that this was my first day off in six weeks. Every single day for those six weeks I had kept going by imagining a day like this hovering just ahead of me, when I could simply *be rather than do*. So many of us are constantly busy, constantly working—we have tough or multiple jobs, families to look after, homes to clean, laundry to fold. We push and strive, only to yearn for the most basic things of all: time, peace, relaxation. Shouldn't we be trying to get as much of that as possible?

There are a few material things that can add to that sense of calm, but plenty that can take away from it. I had been using my stuff to try to create a sanctuary, somewhere I could retreat to and feel safe, content, and like myself. I hadn't appreciated how little I needed in order to do this: basic furniture, some pictures on the walls, a small selection of things that remind me of special moments and people, a couple of bookshelves, and a crappy TV.

Beyond this, things should be obliged to earn their keep. We need to understand that whatever the benefits of each item, they have a cost too: by taking up space in our homes and minds, by costing money to buy and to maintain, and by creating a spiral of desire and dissatisfaction. And ultimately, they can rob us of time—whether that's the hassle of dusting ornaments or the extra hours at work earning money for a shopping habit. Time is key to happiness, and once we lose it, we can never get it back.

When the true cost of stuff is so high, only a few things can be worth it.

A few days after the fire, I was texting some of my pettiest frustrations to a friend. Over those first few days I had passed through sadness and into a stupefied state, as if I had spent all my vitality on tears. I didn't have the energy to think about the heartbreak of losing all my sentimental things, so I became fixated on all the little treats that I had worked, scrimped, and saved for over the years, and which I had now lost. Getting really, really annoyed about that was the only thing that could give me any pep or vim in my gloomy state.

All this went into a series of garbled and venting texts to him. "Oh my GOD I just realized about the COFFEE CUPS GRRR," I tapped out. "And the bloody lamp from my bedroom." A second later I remembered another thing that made me nearly yelp with rage. "And my NUTRIBULLET that I bought as a present to myself when I got this job!! All I wanted was to make an incredibly well-blended smoothie!!!! What joy is left in my sad little life??"

He was very patient and replied to each message with cooing sympathy. The next morning, I arrived at work to find an enormous box on my desk. I opened it. Inside was a Nutribullet, wrapped up with a green ribbon, and a note saying it was from him. I clapped one hand over my mouth and another over my heart, completely taken aback by how generous a gift it was. I called to tell him how grateful I was, and he explained his reasoning: The most precious things I had lost were irreplaceable. But there was nothing wrong with liking a few replaceable things. If silky-smooth smoothies bring you great pleasure, what's wrong with that?

About two years on from the fire, I had dropped any panicked feelings I had about not having enough. I was ready to start trimming around the edges and decided to start with something I can only describe as the "nonsense basket," which I used as a catch-all for things that had no other place, like cases for phones I didn't have any more and promotional tote bags. All these things could be useful in theory, but none of them were things that I needed.

One weekend, I pulled out the tote bags—there were five in total—and started stuffing them with the crap in the basket. I filled the first two with stuff that I could recycle, dropped them by the front door, and put the few things I still needed back into the empty basket. I was quietly thrilled to see that there was no need to root around to find anything. As I picked up the third bag, I thought how annoying it was that I owned these in the first place. Event organizers always hand out the same cotton bags to attendees, which are used to give people leaflets and marketing crap that they don't want. Somehow, by choosing cotton bags that could be used again rather than plastic ones, they give the impression that they care for the environment.

But what help is it for the planet to make so many of these bags that no one needs in the first place?

I stuffed the next three bags with clothes I never wore. Next I went to the kitchen, where I weeded through the overflowing cupboard of mugs and got rid of the ugly ones I had picked up out of necessity soon after the fire, leaving only the ones I actually now used. In the living room I picked up a stack of fifty half-read magazines I had kept in case I ever wanted to finish them, and recycled them all at once. I continued like this for the next hour or so, opening cupboards at random and getting rid of everything that I never used or didn't actually like. So much of it was stuff I had picked up cheaply somewhere, in haste. It represented a time of deep uncertainty and fear, and I was lucky enough to be out of that now.

When I came back from dropping the clothes and mugs at the thrift store, I walked through the flat and looked in at each room. There was plenty of space to move things around in my wardrobe; I could see everything easily in the kitchen cupboards; I could look around and not be bothered by the noise of things I didn't need.

I can never get back the things I have lost. But now I know what it was that I was looking for in the first place. With everything I bought I was trying to make a home for myself, and while some objects helped to do that, a lot did the opposite. I had found balance.

★ ★ ★

In this final chapter, I want to bring together a few themes of this book so far. Some material possessions can bring us happiness, but many don't; we tend to make the best decisions when we take care, rather than acting on autopilot; and our world is so flush with stuff that, unless we think carefully about it, it can easily creep into our lives.

I want to show you that for all the delight that new things can bring, they have a cost too. Some of these costs are obvious, like the literal price. However, even that isn't always fully evident at first; each small impulse buy might be cheap, but collectively they can add up to a problem, with Americans spending an average of $450 a month, or $5,400 a year, by spontaneously buying a few things a week.[1] Other costs, like lost time, are less visible but just as insidious. Because of their cost, if we want to welcome new things into our lives, they should bring us a lot of joy in return.

Some things can bring us proper, lasting pleasure, rather than fleeting joy. We just need to work out what those things are.

Hidden Costs

If I saw a set of tiny shower gels and all-in-one shampoo and conditioners for one pound, I would never, ever buy it. Even if it was fifty pence I wouldn't buy it—my hair feels like sandpaper after using the shampoo, and the bottles are too small to do anything but squirt out the entire contents at once. And yet I just counted up all the tiny, crappy bottles in my bathroom cupboard, and I have seventeen of them. Some are half-used, and some are completely full because the contents are so terrible that I've never even opened themhey just sit there, sometimes falling out of the cupboard when I open the doors, producing a constant low level of irritation.

So what is going on? Why are we so drawn to free stuff that we wouldn't even pay a few pennies for? It's something that researchers call the zero price effect: We act as though something free is worth much more than it is. We are drawn to free things because we see them as having no downside—we get a little bit of value without having to pay anything.

We need to get used to the idea that stuff, whether it's free or not, has a cost. Over 200 million mini toiletries are chucked away every year in the UK, which has a huge environmental impact.[2] There is a further cost to us too. In the one place where we should feel pure relaxation—our own homes—we get stressed because we have filled them with rubbish that we don't need.

More Stuff or More Time?

As we saw when we considered the effects of dopamine, buying new things can bring us short-lived pleasure. But after the novelty has worn off, the pleasure often does too. Our happiness is remarkably constant over time, returning to baseline after we get used to new pleasures. A classic study from 1978 found that even extreme events—like winning the lottery—made no difference to long-term happiness, which dropped back after short-term increases.[3]

So more stuff will probably not bring us lasting pleasure. But it seems that we never get completely accustomed to the joy of having more free time or the stress of having less of it. For example, in 2008 researchers who studied a large longitudinal survey from Germany found that "people who spend more time commuting report lower satisfaction with life, ceteris paribus."[4] People don't get used to the pain of a long commute, or the extra leisure time of a shorter one.

Similarly, a large trial of the four-day work week in the United Kingdom—where people kept the same salary but worked thirty-two hours a week instead of forty—found significant improvements in employee well-being, with 71 percent of workers reporting less burnout after six months.[5] When asked what they did with their day off, the most popular response was "life admin," meaning tasks like chores or grocery shopping, explaining that this allowed them the chance for a "proper break" at the weekend. People had more time to see family and friends, with 62 percent saying that it was easier to combine work with their social life. "One person told us how their 'Sunday dread' had disappeared," said one researcher in the report.

These happiness gains are not surprising when you consider the ten components of a happy life, according to Action for Happiness, a British charity that promotes mental health and well-being. After reviewing copious research, they distilled the things that make happiness most likely into the acronym GREAT DREAM: giving, relating to others, exercising, awareness, trying new things, direction, resilience, emotions, acceptance, and meaning.[6] Stuff might help us to achieve these things—like a pair of roller skates might help us to try something new—but alone it is not enough. For many of us, however, more free time can help with all of this—giving us the chance to see loved ones, take care of our health, and have the space to slow down and reflect.

The link between time and buying stuff was noted by Greg Greiner and Aaron Z. Lewis, two developers inspired by the Time Well Spent movement, which lobbied for tech companies to consider how they attract and exploit users' attention. The movement's reasoning is that our time on earth is too precious to waste on things that are neither productive nor bring us joy.

Greiner and Lewis were inspired by the group and created Time Well $pent—a piece of software that can be installed on your web browser. You input your annual salary, then whenever you are browsing on shopping sites, it converts the prices you see into how much time you would need to work to be able to buy it.

In a blog post, they explained their rather bracing rationale:

> Every week, you sell your time and mental energy to an employer who gives you some money in return. Your paycheck is a literal representation of your time—the scarcest resource in the world. You usually use your time (in the form of money) to buy stuff, but you can also use it to buy freedom. The more dollars you have in your bank account, the more time you can keep to yourself.
>
> What would it be like to buy things with time instead of money? How might we make the relationship between time and money more obvious when you're in the act of shopping?[7]

The post includes a screenshot of the tool in action, showing a top-of-the-range laptop selling for the equivalent of eighteen days, seven hours, and twenty-nine minutes of your labor. Next to it is a slightly less fancy option, which would cost three days, five hours, and forty-nine minutes to work for. After thinking in terms of time cost, the latter suddenly looks a lot more appealing.

This link between stuff and time might feel abstract, but for a certain subculture of people it is anything but. A movement called Financial Independence, Retire Early (FIRE) sprang out of books and blogs in the 2010s encouraging people to save as much money as possible by living frugally and investing the excess.

If they have been able to save enough, then these people retire very early, sometimes even in their thirties.

They deliberately downshift their lifestyles, giving up the luxuries and treats they had previously enjoyed in order to prioritize their freedom in the long term. Sometimes this can result in going drastically against the norm. One of the key voices in this space is a man called Pete Adeney, who runs a blog called *Mr. Money Mustache*, which details how he and his wife managed to save most of their "average" salaries and retire at thirty to start a family. To buy back as much of their time as possible, they reoriented several aspects of their lives around saving money: traveling nearly exclusively by bike, buying groceries from Costco, and ditching fancy phones and cars. He spends a lot of his leisure time walking outside and regularly writes about how happy he is. This might seem like an upheaval if you are surrounded by people who are buying a lot of things.

In one post, he describes something he terms the "California effect," which he observed on a trip to San Francisco. In a city where many people earn sky-high salaries, their concept of what is normal has gone out the window—people might pay $90 an hour for home cleaning and $2,400 a month for car payments, and consider "a $150 bottle of wine to be a reasonable indulgence on a Friday. . . . All of us live in a bubble which we incorrectly perceive as 'normal,'" he writes.[8]

Adeney says that by focusing on taking care of his health, practicing the philosophy of stoicism, and spending plenty of time outside with his family, he can easily feel content living frugally. If that's the case, then that's great. But I can also imagine a world where cutting back so severely could greatly affect your happiness now in the promise of happiness in the future. If you're single and live alone, it's much more important to spend time and money out of the house so that you don't become isolated. Moving to a city with a lower cost of living to save more might not be practical if you have caring responsibilities that tie you to one place. But otherwise, it is a compelling argument for dramatically rethinking how you live and reordering your priorities toward what will actually make you happy in the long term. Who hasn't spent a Sunday night wishing they didn't have to go to work the next day?

Buying Time

Occasionally, something comes along that does allow us to "buy back" time. During the twentieth century, a wealth of new inventions made housework easier and faster. Washing machines meant that laundry could be done in a few hours rather than taking the full day that was previously needed to heat the water, scrub, and wring. Vacuum cleaners meant that floors could be cleaned in minutes rather than the hours of sweeping and beating that were needed before. The time saved by these new innovations was dramatic: Kitchen devices like fridges and electric ovens saved ten hours a week in food preparation time.[9]

Huge changes like this could have freed women from their domestic work, but somehow this didn't happen. In 1920, American full-time housewives did fifty-one hours of housework a week on average. By the 1960s, this had actually increased to fifty-three hours, despite the proliferation of new devices.[10] When housework became easier, standards got higher. Instead of banking the saved time for leisure, American women instead shifted their attention to other tasks around the home.

My mother and her two sisters tell a story that illustrates how the "time-saving" devices of the twentieth century affected housework in their own home. When my oldest aunt was a child, she would have clean underwear every few days, but my mother, who is the youngest, wore fresh ones every day. It would have been too much for my grandmother to hand-wash enough clothes for her children to wear new things every day, but as soon as a washing machine made it possible, it happened. My grandmother didn't take the time saved and use it for herself, but instead spent some of it doing more washing than before. Now that more cleaning was possible, the bar for something being "clean enough" was raised.

Today, those of us lucky enough to live in rich parts of the world are mostly desensitized to the time-saving powers of these inventions. But sometimes their incredible effects are made clear, as happened when I first moved to a flat with a dishwasher. To begin with, the amount of time it saved was extraordinary—after dinner it took just five minutes to clear up, meaning I could spend more time relaxing. But soon, of course, the work expanded to fill the vacancy. I would leave mugs around the house, picking a clean one from the cupboard every time I wanted a cup of tea, rather than reusing the same one to save washing up.

Some people might describe this expansion of work as an example of Parkinson's Law, a theory put forward by C. Northcote Parkinson, a British civil servant, in an article in *The Economist* in 1955. Through observing how the bureaucracy worked, he postulated that "work expands so as to fill the time available for its completion."

I think there's a slightly better way of looking at this effect: Instead of work expanding, it's an example of our wants expanding. When machines allow us to easily reach a certain level of cleanliness, we are no longer satisfied with what we had before. I therefore want to pose a slightly tweaked version of Parkinson's Law: Our desires expand to fill the resources we have available.

Time-saving devices have the potential to bring us enormous amounts of pleasure, if we use them wisely. If you can fiercely guard your time and know exactly how you will use your new freedom—even if that is just lying in bed reading—then it is well worth buying something that truly can save you a lot of time. Otherwise, be warned that unguarded time can easily be filled with yet more work.

Pausing Before You Buy

As you might have noticed, there is one point that I keep returning to: Buying (and owning) on autopilot tends not to make us happy, but being deliberate and mindful sometimes can. The former can lead to clutter, financial difficulties, and a belief that how we currently are is not good enough, while the latter can help us to express ourselves and find pleasure in a healthy way.

I want us to think about the things that bring us true, lasting pleasure almost as the opposite to the approach discussed in the first chapter—buying driven by impulse and fleeting joy. Slow, mindful purchases are the sort we have thought through, and considered the true cost of, before deciding they're worth it. Purchases like these bring joy to our lives for a long time and are seldom regretted.

One way of thinking about these two types of purchases could be with the System 1 and System 2 theory put forward in *Thinking Fast and Slow* by Daniel Kahneman, a psychologist whose work we looked at in chapter seven. It refers to two different modes in which our minds can operate: making snap decisions based on impulse and emotions (System 1), or thinking things through and making choices based on reason that consider long-term impacts (System 2). While dopamine-led impulse buying might be done by System 1 thinking, it is the slower, considered purchases made by System 2 that will bring us lasting joy.

While System 2 can make better decisions, it doesn't work as quickly as System 1. Often, to see something rationally, we need time to step back from our emotions and impulses. In that time, we can deliberately engage the logical mind by setting ourselves some questions.

With hindsight, it's usually clear which items were good purchases and which were not. After a few months, the glitter of novelty will have worn off, and the true costs of upkeep and storage will be apparent. There are a few questions you can ask yourself to test whether something was a good purchase when you've owned it for, say, a year. Firstly, if you lost this item, would you race back out to buy another one? If yes, it is bringing something positive to your life, but if no, perhaps it isn't bringing enough joy to warrant the financial and time costs. Secondly, with everything you know about this object now, does the price still seem good? Good purchases can feel like a total bargain in terms of the amount of pleasure they bring, while others seem like a waste of money after a period of time.

By way of example, here are some things that pass these tests with flying colors for me:

- A good eye mask and earplugs: I suffered from severe and relentless insomnia for a year and a half in my midtwenties. It was more than being tired—I was so zonked out that it felt like I was looking at the world through the end of a long bottle, seeing everything in slight distortion. I struggled to focus enough to follow a conversation or remember basic things. Ultimately, I had to get rid of the sources of stress in my life to fully recover, but along the way, getting a decent eye mask and earplugs helped a lot. I found a mask that had scooped cups over the eyes to ensure total darkness, and silicone earplugs that mold to the shape of your ears. Together they give me an extra hour or so of sleep a day—completely changing my life for less than fifteen pounds.

- My laptop: At £300 (about $378), it was the second-cheapest one in the shop. But it is light enough to carry in a handbag and works fine for writing and watching TV, things that I do every day.
- Running leggings with a pocket: I like to run in my local park but find it incredibly annoying to have to carry my phone and keys in my hands. The leggings with a pocket make the experience much more pleasant, and they even help me run faster, as I can properly use my arms.
- A black roll-neck top: It makes me look falsely sophisticated and goes with everything. I don't care what brand it is (unlike Steve Jobs).

These are items that make my life truly better. They don't bring the life-changing happiness of more free time or being around people I love, but they help. And most of the time, I think that is the best that we can hope for with our stuff.

★ ★ ★

This chapter is short for a reason. There aren't many material things that will bring you real pleasure, the feeling that lasts long after the initial dopamine thrill has worn away.

If we want to work out which things will give us a short-lived thrill and which will improve our lives in the long run, we can't rely on a gut feeling. Write down what you want and come back to it in a few days or a month. Sleep on a decision to buy something. Close the tabs on your phone and see, at the end of the day, if you can remember what you were looking at. Acting immediately means letting our impulses control what we do, impulses that have been shaped by our desire for social status and distraction, by our urge to control the future while never parting with the past, by advertising and pressure and stress.

While our desire for new stuff is infinite, the benefits it can bring are not.

FINAL THOUGHTS

I hope that if you take one thing away from this book, it is the confidence to feel that you can take control of what you own. You buy things—and put a large amount of time and effort into looking after them—in order to improve your life. If they are not doing that, you do not have to keep them. The things that are most likely to bring benefits are the ones that will bring pleasure over a long period, and not just fleeting thrills in the instant. Given that the cost of stuff is so high (both for individuals and for the planet), the benefits should be too.

TIME AND MONEY CONVERSIONS

It's worthwhile to think about the things you buy in terms of work time. If you are paid by the hour, it will be easy to calculate the time cost of an item by dividing its cost by your hourly wage. If you know your annual salary, then try this method instead. Take 260 (the number of weekdays in a year) and subtract the number of vacation days and public holidays you have. Divide your annual salary by that number to find how much you're paid for each day of work, and divide that by the number of hours you work in a day to find your hourly rate.

For example, if you earn $60,000 a year and live in the United States, where you work about 250 days a year, then your daily rate is $60,000/250 = $240. If you work eight hours a day, then your hourly pay is $30. If you're thinking of buying a new coat that's $300, then you would have to work 1.25 days to earn it. A good-quality coat that will keep you cozy for years is probably worth putting in an extra few days at work, but one that's part of this week's micro trend and will be outdated by next winter might not be.

How much time are you spending looking after things?

Next you can think about the amount of time you spend looking after the things that you already own. Over a week, note down every time you stop to take care of your possessions. This could be half an hour to take a jacket to the dry cleaner, ten minutes of dusting decorations on the mantelpiece, or an hour spent rubbing polish into your dining table. At the end of the week, add it up, excluding time spent doing unavoidable things like washing up after a meal or cleaning the bathroom. In some weeks this can add up to several hours, creating another half or full day of work to the week.

Imagine going back to when you bought those items. How would it feel if, next to the price on the tag, there was also the amount of time it would cost to look after the thing? Would it still be worth buying? You can even use the exercise above to quantify this. If you buy a $100 pair of shoes that need half an hour of polishing once a month, you can calculate a true cost for them by adding in your labor cost. If your hourly pay works out to $30 as above, then the shoes are actually $100 upfront with an additional $15 monthly subscription cost. Is that still a good deal?

Thinking about the time cost of upkeep has had a radical effect on the things that I now choose to buy. I absolutely loathe ironing, and for me there is absolutely no item of clothing nice enough to warrant ten minutes of steaming it for each wear. Similarly, I hate hand-washing clothes—it feels like an extraordinarily annoying use of time given that we invented washing machines a hundred years ago. Because of this, I will never again buy anything made of linen because of the constant, constant ironing, and I check laundry labels whenever I'm out shopping and put down anything that can't go in the washing machine. Life is too short to be hand-washing your underwear.

The Random Box

I had been in the new flat for about a year when the mystery of what was in the "RANDOM" box finally got to me. As my life recovered, my need for magical thinking lessened, until it was overtaken by an irresistible curiosity. I couldn't wait any longer to find out what was inside. I tore into the box with my hands, not even waiting to find a pair of scissors.

The contents were not quite as I expected.

Quite a lot of it was useless, the sort of stuff that I should have thrown away years ago but never quite got round to, which explains how it ended up getting chucked into a box marked "random" in the first place.

There was a poem written to me by my first boyfriend when we were teenagers, which had rhymed "I love you to bits" with something . . . rude. There was a cheap fridge magnet I had bought on vacation in Spain, which must have been the thing I could hear clunking around in the box. The papery rustling, I discovered, was a cache of old water bills I hadn't needed for years. And then there was a box of notecards printed with the American painter Edward Hopper's lonely figures, which had always been too dreary to send to anyone.

That was it. That was all I had left to remind me of my life before that point. I first sighed with disappointment, then started laughing. I couldn't believe I had treated this box with so much reverence, as if it would hold the answers to all my longing. Of course the things I cared about had gone—they couldn't have all fit into one box! Anything else was wishful, stupid thinking.

The light in the room seemed brighter as I saw what was in front of me. There was no box that could hold everything I wanted, no collection of bits and bobs that would let me return to the past, no set of objects that would make me feel forever content or beautiful or important. We can choose things that please us or help us to feel that yesterday wasn't so long ago. If chosen smartly, they can please us for a while, but they will never be the center of our lives.

I looked again at what was in the box. The mementos were not from the happiest days of my life, or the most important, but instead just a random cross-section of days that I had lived. It was the true memory box, in a way: an honest reflection of my life told through the day-to-day. There was love, mundanity, rubbish, and fun. That was it.

Notes

INTRODUCTION

1.   Valentina Portela, "The Fashion Industry Waste Is Drastically Contributing to Climate Change," *CALPIRG*, March 9, 2021, https://pirg.org/california/articles/the-fashion-industry-waste-is-drastically-contributing-to-climate-change/.

2.   "Ten-Year-Olds Have £7,000 Worth of Toys but Play with Just £330," Telegraph, October 20, 2010, https://www.telegraph.co.uk/finance/newsbysector/retailandconsumer/8074156/Ten-year-olds-have-7000-worth-of-toys-but-play-with-just-330.html#:~:text=A%20typical%20child%20owns%20238,their%20children%20never%20play%20with.

3.   Kendra Mangione, "Shirtless Man Uses Belt as a Whip Outside Vancouver Black Friday Sale," *CTV News*, November 27, 2016, https://bc.ctvnews.ca/shirtless-man-uses-belt-as-a-whip-outside-vancouver-black-friday-sale-1.3179008; and Lynne Moore, "Girl Trampled in Black Friday Wal-Mart Rush," *MLive*, November 25, 2011, https://www.mlive.com/news/muskegon/2011/11/girl_trampled_in_black_friday.html.

4.   "Almost Half of Brits Don't Remember What They Got for Christmas Last Year," *Doncaster Free Press*, December 20, 2018, https://www.doncasterfreepress.co.uk/news/almost-half-of-brits-dont-remember-what-they-got-for-christmas-last-year-43462.

LESSON 1: SATISFACTION ISN'T FOUND WHILE SHOPPING

1. Victor H. Denenberg, Douglas S. Kim, and Richard D. Palmiter, "The Role of Dopamine in Learning, Memory, and Performance of a Water Escape Task," *Behavioural Brain Research* 148, no. 1–2 (January 2004): 73–78, https://doi.org/10.1016/S0166-4328(03)00183-9.

2. "Volume and Consumption: How Much Does the World Buy?," *Common Objective*, May 14, 2018, https://www.commonobjective.co/article/volume -and-consumption-how-much-does-the-world-buy.

3. "Volume and Consumption."

4. Rebecca Starkins, "How Much Clothing Did an 18th-Century Woman Really Own?," Colonial Williamsburg, last modified August 10, 2020, https://www.colonialwilliamsburg.org/learn/living-history/how-much -clothing-did-18th-century-woman-really-own/.

5. Braudel, Fernand, *Civilization and Capitalism, 15th–18th Century: Vol. 1, The Structure of Everyday Life*, Berkeley, CA: University of California Press, 1992, 315.

6. Julia B. Edwards, Alan C. McKinnon, and Sharon L. Cullinane, "Comparative Analysis of the Carbon Footprints of Conventional and Online Retailing: A 'Last Mile' Perspective," *International Journal of Physical Distribution & Logistics Management* 40, no. 1/2 (February 2010): 103–23, https://doi.org/10.1108/09600031011018055

7. Optoro Inc., 2019 *Impact Report*, 2020, https://info.optoro.com/hubfs /Optoro%202019%20Impact%20Report.pdf.

8. Malin Sundström, Sara Hjelm-Lidholm, and Anita Radon, "Clicking the Boredom Away—Exploring Impulse Fashion Buying Behavior Online," *Journal of Retailing and Consumer Services* 47 (March 2019): 150–56, https://doi.org/10.1016/j.jretconser.2018.11.006.

9. Peter Grinspoon, MD, "Dopamine Fasting: Misunderstanding Science Spawns a Maladaptive Fad," *Harvard Health Publishing*, February 26, 2020, https://www.health.harvard.edu/blog/dopamine-fasting-misunderstanding -science-spawns-a-maladaptive-fad-2020022618917.

LESSON 2: YOU ARE MORE THAN YOUR THINGS

1. Vanek Smith and Sindhu Gnanasambandan, "Episode 672: Bagging a Birkin," December 25, 2015, in *Planet Money*, podcast, transcript, https://www.npr.org/transcripts/460870534.

2. Shankar Vedantam, Maggie Penman, Rhaina Cohen, and Tara Boyle, "Never go to Vegas," March 18, 2019, in *Hidden Brain: A Conversation about Life's Unseen Patterns*, produced by Shankar Vedantam, Maggie Penman, Rhaina Cohen, and Tara Boyle, podcast, transcript, https://www.npr.org/transcripts/704416322?storyId=704416322?storyId=704416322.

3. Olivia Hosken, "Gwyneth Paltrow Hired a Personal Book Curator—Here's What He Chose for Her Shelves," *Town & Country*, August 20, 2019, https://www.townandcountrymag.com/style/home-decor/a28680227/how-to-organize-books-thatcher-wine-gwyneth-paltrow/.

4. Darwin Correspondence Project, "Letter no. 2743: Charles Darwin to Asa Gray, April 3, 1860," accessed on November 2, 2023, https://www.darwinproject.ac.uk/letter/DCP-LETT-2743.xml.

5. Christopher R. von Rueden et al., "Political Influence Associates with Cortisol and Health among Egalitarian Forager-Farmers," *Evolution, Medicine, and Public Health* 2014, no. 1 (September 2014): 122–33, https://doi.org/10.1093/emph/eou021.

6. Alice Moran, "Uniform Debate," YouGov, last modified June 29, 2011, https://yougov.co.uk/society/articles/1982-uniform-debate?redirect_from=%2Fnews%2F2011%2F06%2F29%2Funiform-debate%2F.

7. Cameron Anderson et al., "The Local-Ladder Effect: Social Status and Subjective Well-Being," *Psychological Science* 23, no. 7 (May 2012): 764–71, https://doi.org/10.1177/09567976114345.

LESSON 3: PLENTIFUL THINGS AREN'T WORTHLESS

1. Meng Zhu, Rebecca K. Ratner, "Scarcity Polarizes Preferences: The Impact on Choice among Multiple Items in a Product Class," *Journal of Marketing Research* 52, no. 1 (February 2015): 13–26, https://doi.org/10.1509/jmr.13.0451.

2. Anuj K. Shah, Sendhil Mullainathan, and Eldar Shafir, "Some Consequences of Having Too Little," *Science* 338, no. 6107 (November 2012): 682–85, https://www.science.org/doi/10.1126/science.1222426.

3. Raymond Zhong, "Alibaba Reports Slower Sales Growth for Its Singles Day Shopping Event," *New York Times*, November 11, 2021, https://www.nytimes.com/2021/11/11/technology/alibaba-singles-day-sales.html.

4. International Monetary Fund, "Real GDP Growth," accessed on October 1, 2023, https://www.imf.org/external/datamapper/NGDPD@W EO/ LKA?zoom=LK A&highlight=LKA.

5. Timothy C. Brock, "Implications of Commodity Theory for Value Change," in *Psychological Foundations of Attitudes*, ed. Greenwald and Brock (New York: Academic Press, 1968).

6.   Howard L. Fromkin, "Effects of Experimentally Aroused Feelings of Undistinctiveness upon Valuation of Scarce and Novel Experiences," *Journal of Personality and Social Psychology* 16, no. 3 (1970): 521–29, https://doi.org /10.1037/h0030059.

7.   Elizabeth Paton, "The $50 Dress That Conquered Britain," *New York Times*, July 11, 2019, https://www.nytimes.com/2019/07/11/fashion/uk-the -dress-zara.html.

8.   Joan Didion, *The White Album* (New York: Simon & Schuster, 1979).

9.   Brian Stelter, "Tape Delay by NBC Faces End Run by Online Fans," *New York Times*, August 8, 2008, https://www.nytimes.com/2008/08/09 /sports/olympics/09nbc.html.

10.   Anthony D. Miyazaki, Alexandra Aguirre Rodriguez, and Jeff Langenderfer, "Price, Scarcity, and Consumer Willingness to Purchase Pirated Media Products," *Journal of Public Policy & Marketing* 28, no. 1 (April 2009): 71–84, https://doi.org/10.1509/jppm.28.1.71.

11.   Sharon S. Brehm and Marsha Weinraub, "Physical Barriers and Psychological Reactance: 2-Yr-Olds' Responses to Threats to Freedom," *Journal of Personality and Social Psychology* 35, no. 11 (1977): 830–36, https://doi.org/10.1037/0022-3514.35.11.830.

12.   Shah, Mullainathan, and Shafir, "Having Too Little," 682–85.

LESSON 4: YOU ARE NOT WHAT YOU OWN

1.   Maya Ernest, "What Is Ironic Fashion, and Why Is TikTok Obsessed with It?," *Input*, June 7, 2022, https://www.inverse.com/input/style/what-is -ironic-fashion-tiktok-trend-ogbff-interview-t-shirts.

2.   "Everything You Need to Know about the Claddagh Ring," Irish Family History Centre, accessed October 20, 2023, https://www .irishfamilyhistorycentre.com/article/everything-about-claddagh-ring/.

3.   S. Craig Roberts, Roy C. Owen, and Jan Havlicek, "Distinguishing between Perceiver and Wearer Effects in Clothing Color-Associated Attributions," *Evolutionary Psychology* 8, no. 3 (September 2010): 350–64, https://doi.org/10.1177/147470491000800304.

4.   Mark G. Frank and Thomas Gilovich, "The Dark Side of Self- and Social Perception: Black Uniforms and Aggression in Professional Sports," *Journal of Personality and Social Psychology* 54, no. 1 (January 1988): 74–85, https://doi.org/10.1037/0022-3514.54.1.74.

5.   Russell A. Hill and Robert A. Barton, "Red Enhances Human Performance in Contests," *Nature* 435, no. 293 (May 2005): https://doi.org /10.1038/435293a.

6. Jennifer L. Bonnet and Benjamin McAlexander, "First Impressions and the Reference Encounter: The Influence of Affect and Clothing on Librarian Approachability," *Journal of Academic Librarianship* 39, no. 4 (July 2013): 335–46, https://doi.org/10.1016/j.acalib.2012.11.025.

7. Leonard Bickman, "The Effect of Social Status on the Honesty of Others," *Journal of Social Psychology* 85 (1971): 87–92, https://doi.org/10.1080/00224545.1971.9918547.

8. Soae L.Paek, "Effect of Garment Style on the Perception of Personal Traits," *Clothing and Textiles Research Journal* 5 no. 1 (September 1986): 10–16, https://doi.org/10.1177/0887302X8600500102.

9. "About Graceland," Graceland.com, accessed October 1, 2023, https://www.graceland.com/about-graceland.

10. Grace Cook, "Rooms of Their Own," *Financial Times*, April 22, 2022, https://www.ft.com/content/74c530ac-304f-4905-a457-d0bb5837007f.

LESSON 5: COLLECTING IS MORE THAN BUYING STUFF

1. Shirley M. Mueller, *Inside the Head of a Collector* (Seattle: Lucia Marquand, 2019).

2. Shirley M. Mueller, "Letting Go," *Fine Art Connoisseur* 19, no. 5 (October 2022): 92–93, https://issuu.com/thomaselmo/docs/facsepoct2022_digital.

3. Jens Kleine, Thomas Peschke, and Niklas Wagner, "Collectors: Personality between Consumption and Investment," *Journal of Behavioral and Experimental Finance* 32 (December 2021): https://doi.org/10.1016/j.jbef.2021.100566.

4. Mary K. Jacob, "This Viral House on Zillow Has a Disturbing Amount of Storage Space," *New York Post*, July 14, 2022, https://nypost.com/2022/07/13/this-viral-house-has-a-disturbing-amount-of-storage-space/.

5. Steven W. Anderson, Hanna Damasio, and Antonio R. Damasio, "A Neural Basis for Collecting Behaviour in Humans," *Brain* 128, no. 1 (January 2005): 201–12, https://doi.org/10.1093/brain/awh329.

6. American Psychiatric Association, "What Is Hoarding Disorder?," APA, last updated August 2021, https://www.psychiatry.org/patients-families/hoarding-disorder/what-is-hoarding-disorder.

7. National Health Service, "Hoarding Disorder," NHS, last updated June 1, 2022, https://www.nhs.uk/mental-health/conditions/hoarding-disorder/.

8. "SI-R: Saving Inventory—Revised," CGA Toolkit Plus, accessed October 1, 2023, https://www.cgakit.com/ho-2-si-r.

9. Sara A. Luchian, Richard J. McNally, and Jill M. Hooley, "Cognitive Aspects of Nonclinical Obsessive-Compulsive Hoarding," *Behaviour Research and Therapy* 45, no. 7 (July 2007): 1657–62, https://doi.org/10.1016/j.brat.2006.08.014.

LESSON 6: YOU CAN'T HOLD ON TO EVERY MEMORY

1. R. Quian Quiroga et al., "Invariant Visual Representation by Single Neurons in the Human Brain," *Nature* 435, no. 1102–1107 (June 2005): https://doi.org/10.1038/nature03687.

2. Sarah F. Brosnan et al., "Endowment Effects in Chimpanzees," *Current Biology* 17, no. 19 (October 2007): 1704–707, https://doi.org/10.1016/j.cub.2007.08.059.

3. Christopher Brett Jaeger et al., "Predicting Variation in Endowment Effect Magnitudes," *Evolution and Human Behavior* 41, no. 3 (May 2020): 253–59, https://doi.org/10.1016/j.evolhumbehav.2020.04.002.

4. Maarten C. Eisma et al., "Rumination, Worry and Negative and Positive Affect in Prolonged Grief: A Daily Diary Study," *Clinical Psychology & Psychotherapy* 29, no. 1 (January 2022): https://doi.org/10.1002/cpp.2635.

5. Julia W. Felton, David A. Cole, and Nina C. Martin," Effects of Rumination on Child and Adolescent Depressive Reactions to a Natural Disaster: The 2010 Nashville Flood," *Journal of Abnormal Psychology* 122, no 1 (February 2013): 64–73, https://doi.org/10.1037/a0029303.

6. Krystine Irene Batcho, "The Nostalgia Inventory," accessed November 2, 2023, https://www.cbsnews.com/htdocs/pdf/Batcho_Nostalgia_Inventory.pdf.

7. Krystine Irene Batcho, "Nostalgia: Retreat or Support in Difficult Times?," *The American Journal of Psychology* 126, no. 3 (October 2013): 355–67, https://doi.org/10.5406/amerjpsyc.126.3.0355.

LESSON 7: YOU MIGHT NOT NEED THAT

1. Amos Tversky and Daniel Kahneman, "Judgment under Uncertainty: Heuristics and Biases," *Science* 185, no. 4157 (September 1974): 1124–31, https://www.science.org/doi/10.1126/science.185.4157.1124.

2. Paco Underhill, *Why We Buy: The Science of Shopping* (New York: Simon & Schuster, 1999).

3. Deborah A. Cohen and Susan H. Babey, "Candy at the Cash Register: A Risk Factor for Obesity and Chronic Disease," *The New England Journal of Medicine* 367, no. 15 (October 2012): 1381–3, https://www.nejm.org/doi/full/10.1056/nejmp1209443#.

4. Peter Walker, "Unhealthy Snacks to Be Banned from Checkouts at Supermarkets in England," *Guardian* (US edition), December 28, 2020, https://www.theguardian.com/business/2020/dec/28/unhealthy-snacks-to-be-banned-from-checkouts-supermarkets-in-england.

LESSON 8: BEAUTY IS NECESSARY

1. See Ipsos MORI's survey: *People and Places: Public Attitudes to Beauty* (London: Ipsos MORI, 2010), https://www.designcouncil.org.uk/fileadmin/uploads/dc/Documents/people-and-places.pdf.

2. J. H. Bernard, trans., *Kant's Critique of Judgement*, 2nd ed. (London: Macmillan, 1914), https://oll.libertyfund.org/titles/bernard-the-critique-of-judgement.

3. See, for example, John D. Balling and John H. Falk, "Development of Visual Preference for Natural Environments," *Environment and Behavior* 14, no. 1 (January 1982): 5–28, https://doi.org/10.1177/0013916582141001.

4. "Indoor Plants Market Size to Reach USD 30.4 Billion by 2032 growing at 6.6% CAGR." Acumen Research and Consulting. https://www.acumenresearchandconsulting.com/press-releases/indoor-plants-market.

5. So-Young Park et al., "Effects of Interior Plantscapes on Indoor Environments and Stress Level of High School Students," *Journal of the Japanese Society for Horticultural Science* 77, no. 4 (October 2008): 447–54, https://www.jstage.jst.go.jp/article/jjshs1/77/4/77_4_447/_pdf.

6. Miguel de Seixas, David Williamson, Gemma Barker, and Ruth Vickerstaff, "Horticultural Therapy in a Psychiatric In-Patient Setting," *The British Journal of Psychiatry International* 14, no. 4 (November 2017): 87–89, https://doi.org/10.1192/S2056474000002087.

7. Norma Daykin et al., "Review: The Impact of Art, Design and Environment in Mental Healthcare: A Systematic Review of the Literature," *Journal of the Royal Society for the Promotion of Health* 128, no. 2 (March 2008): 85–94, https://doi.org/10.1177/1466424007087806.

8. María Luisa Martínez-Martí, María José Hernández-Lloreda, and María Dolores Avia, MD, "Appreciation of Beauty and Excellence: Relationship with Personality, Prosociality and Well-Being," *Journal of Happiness Studies: An Interdisciplinary Forum on Subjective Well-Being* 17, no. 6 (December 2016): 2613–34; https://doi.org/10.1007/s10902-015-9709-6.

9. Christopher Peterson and Martin Seligman, *Character Strengths and Virtues: A Handbook and Classification* (Oxford: OUP, 2004).

10. Rhett Diessner et al., "Beauty and Hope: A Moral Beauty Intervention," *Journal of Moral Education* 35, no. 3 (2006): 301–17, https://doi.org/10.1080/03057240600874430.

11. Isla MacFarlane, "Survey Suggests Brits Harbour Negative Perceptions about New Builds," *Showhouse*, October 2, 2019, https://www.showhouse .co.uk/news/survey-suggests-brits-harbour-negative-perceptions-about-new -builds/.

12. Rowan Moore, "St Pancras Renaissance Hotel: The Rebirth of a Gothic Masterpiece," *Guardian* (US edition), February 12, 2011, https://www .theguardian.com/artanddesign/2011/feb/13/midland-grand-hotel-st -pancras.

13. Jennifer L, Roberts, "The Power of Patience," *Harvard Magazine*, November-December 2013, https://www.harvardmagazine.com/2013/10 /the-power-of-patience.

14. "Nature and Mental Health: How Can Nature Benefit My Mental Health?," Mind, November 2021, https://www.mind.org.uk/information -support/tips-for-everyday-living/nature-and-mental-health/how-nature -benefits-mental-health/.

15. Claudia C. Collins, Angela M. O'Callaghan, "The Impact of Horticultural Responsibility on Health Indicators and Quality of Life in Assisted Living," *HortTechnology* 18, no. 4 (October 2008): 611–18, https://doi.org/10.21273/HORTTECH.18.4.611.

LESSON 9: TRUE PLEASURE LASTS

1. Sarah O'Brien, "Consumers Cough Up $5,400 a Year on Impulse Purchases," CNBC, February 23, 2018, https://www.cnbc.com/2018/02/23 /consumers-cough-up-5400-a-year-on-impulse-purchases.html.

2. Yossi Sheffi, "Removing Mini-Shampoos from Hotel Rooms Won't Save the Environment," *The MIT Press Reader*, August 23, 2019. https://thereader .mitpress.mit.edu/ plastics- crisis- balancing- green/.

3. Philip Brickman, Dan Coates, and Ronnie Janoff-Bulman, "Lottery Winners and Accident Victims: Is Happiness Relative?," *Journal of Personality and Social Psychology* 36, no. 8 (August 1978): 917–27, https://doi.org/10.1037 /0022-3514.36.8.917.

4. Alois Stutzer, Bruno S. Frey, "Stress That Doesn't Pay: The Commuting Paradox," *The Scandinavian Journal of Economics* 110, no. 2 (June 2008): 339–66, http://www.jstor.org/stable/25195346.

5. Fred Lewsey, "Would You Prefer a Four-Day Working Week?," University of Cambridge, February 21, 2023, https://www.cam.ac.uk/stories /fourdayweek.

6. "10 Keys to Happier Living," Action for Happiness, accessed November 2, 2023, https://actionforhappiness.org/10-keys.

7. Aaron Z. Lewis, "Introducing Time Well $pent," *AZL.BLOG*, April 30, 2018, https://aaronzlewis.com/blog/2018/04/30/time-well-spent/.

8. "The California Effect," *Mr. Money Mustache* (blog), December 10, 2022, https://www.mrmoneymustache.com/2022/12/10/the-california-effect/.

9. Juliet Schor, *The Overworked American: The Unexpected Decline of Leisure* (New York: Basic Books, 1992).

10. Schor, *The Overworked American*.

Acknowledgments

I am indebted to the following people for helping to turn a clutch of thoughts into the book you're holding. Paul Clements, you are a brilliant editor and a lot of fun. Thank you for commissioning the original feature that set off the series of events that led here. Thank you to Tamsin English for your help shaping my thoughts in the early stages. Thank you to my agent, Sarah Williams, for your guidance and patience; your instant enthusiasm for the book kept me going through the doldrums of lockdown. Thank you to Nicola Crane and Jessica Lacey for your close reading and sharp ideas, without which this would be a very different book.

Thank you to the editorial, design, and production teams at Octopus, who turned a Google Doc into a book, and to the marketing and publicity teams, who got the book into your hands. Thank you also to my copyeditor, Susanne Hillen, and proofreader, Tania Charles. Thank you very much to the team at Chronicle Books who safely ferried this book across the Atlantic and into the US. Thanks to my lovely editor Cara Bedick, who saw something in the book and suggested ways to tweak it for a new audience, and the trusty team of copyeditors, including Mary Paplham and Maya Wechsler.

Thank you to all the academics who spared their time to be interviewed, and to those who shared personal stories that have helped to bring that expertise to life. They include Professor Cameron Anderson, Professor Krystine Batcho, Professor Anjan Chatterjee, Sian Clarke, Demetria and Johannes, Professor Joseph Ferrari, Katie Hart, Dr. Samuel Hughes, Professor Owen Jones, Megan Karnes, Isabelle Kennedy, Professor Brian Knutson, Professor Feng Li, Professor Ciara McCabe, Jake McKenzie, Dr. Shirley Mueller, Dr. Caroline Roux, Professor Gail Steketee, Professor Jill Sundie, Paco Underhill, Simonne Waud, Sister Monica Williams, and Colin Wright.

Thank you to the friends who have already graciously appeared in the pages of this book, whether directly or obliquely: Amanda Cashmore, Imogen Jain, Isabelle Keenan, Millie Kershaw, Alex Ma, and Ayonija Sundararajan. And to those who have not yet appeared but have been steadfast through the vicissitudes of writing, thank you to Hannah Galley, Izzy Lyons, Katie Wagstaff, and Faye White. Special thanks to Claudia Summers, who took care of multiple practical things around the house while I was writing. I loved writing side-by-side with you in your (our) local.

Thank you to the members of the Creative And Riting Association Club [*sic*]—Mimi Launder, Cara McGoogan, Luke Mintz, Harriet Pavey, Helena Pike, and Tom Rees. Your feedback has been both helpful and tactful. I also thought it wise to put you in here given that now it's only polite for you to put me in your own acknowledgments pages. And thank you, Francis Dearnley, the Virgil to my Dante. Inferno to Infernos.

Of course, many, many thanks to Frank Lawton, whose open ear and absorbent shoulder were indispensable in the final months of this book's gestation.

Most fundamental thanks go to my family. My granny Eirlys Chandler always showed us the joy of books. My parents provided me with plenty to read, and with enough clean notebooks to practice writing (as long as you hid them from Dad, who would otherwise scrawl equations in them). Thank you to Rosie: Out of all the sisters in the world, you are one of them. You have given me plenty to write about over the years.

Thank you also to my family for instilling certain attitudes in me that were crucial for writing this. If there is a Chandler-Wilde philosophy, it is to laugh when things go wrong—which they often do. If you have been trained to laugh at missed buses, lost keys, and wonky shelves, it becomes easier to weather true adversity, to find heartbreak suddenly collapsing into bathos. Tears and laughter come together. Lemonade is made in great quantities.

About the Author

Helen Chandler-Wilde is a news and features journalist who has worked at Bloomberg, *The Telegraph*, and the BBC amongst other outlets. She studied social sciences and languages at UCL and has a master's degree in journalism.

On New Year's Eve 2018 she lost nearly all her possessions in a fire at a storage unit in London.

She lives in south London. This is her first book.